Meghan Markle and Kate Middleton

The Wives of Windsor - 2 Books in 1

Katy Holborn and Michael Woodford

Table of Contents

Meghan Markle

A Meghan Markle Biography

Katy Holborn

I. Introduction: A Cinderella Story for the Internet Age

In 2017, American cable television actress Meghan Markle topped Google's annual list of the most searched actors of the year. This would be her second year in a row. She bested, for example, the likes of box office record-breaking Wonder Woman, Gal Gadot, and the living legend herself, multiple Academy Award winner Meryl Streep. Compared to these two names, Ms. Markle's acting resume is thin. As a matter of fact, for many people, she seemed to have come out of nowhere.

Only a handful of things can propel a person from relative obscurity to a name in lights. Even little girls all over the world would know the answer to this – a dashing Prince Charming must have found his Cinderella against all odds. They will marry in a beautiful, lavish ceremony before an adoring public and live happily ever after.

Indeed, Meghan Markle's climb to the top of this list and in the minds of the international public is largely credited to her relationship with the United Kingdom's beloved Prince Harry – a romance confirmed on November 2016, and with an engagement announced a year later on November 2017.

That anything relating to Prince Harry is interesting on a global scale comes as no surprise. He is one of the iconic and captivating, late Princess Diana's two sons. The world sympathetically rode along with him and his older brother, Prince William, in the rollercoaster of their parents' tumultuous relationship and ultimately, their mother's tragic death. But the brothers were captivating on their own merits. Prince William had married his own "Cinderella," the much adored Kate Middleton, and they gave birth to beautiful children. Prince Harry, on the other hand, was fascinating for his party boy image and string of romantic entanglements. These modern, young royals were like a breath of fresh air in an old institution, and everything they did was under such scrutiny it was like living under a microscope. When he and Meghan started dating in 2016 and the relationship looked to be very serious, that attention only intensified.

Because their love story isn't just about a mysterious, beautiful, young woman walking into a room and sweeping Prince Charming off his feet. In the Internet Age, the mystery around "Cinderella" can be vanquished with a few strokes of the keyboard.

Search Meghan Markle – as millions over millions of people have in 2016, 2017 and thereafter - and it is immediately clear that this "Cinderella" is a woman with history and complexity. She is her own person – not a blank slate to be transformed by a fairy godmother, not a cinder girl seeking salvation, not a barefoot awaiting fancy shoes to fill.

Minutes or even seconds into one's search, and it is revealed she is older than Prince Harry by a couple of years. A little surprising, but rumors of the prince dating older women was not new. A few more search results and one might discover she is half-black– outrageous to some sad minds in dark corners of the Internet, but she and Prince Harry wouldn't be the first mixed-race royal couple. European aristocracies like the Habsburgs boast of such modern romances, and intriguingly, there is a popular but unproven theory that Queen Charlotte, wife of King George III and grandmother to Queen Victoria, may have been biracial herself.

Search a bit more, and Ms. Markle's largest claim to individual fame is that she was a series regular on the hit American cable show, Suits. That's all right, one might think. Actresses and royalty have often been linked to the most curious results. Sometimes controversial - as in the case of comic stage actress Nell Gwyn, beloved mistress of King Charles II in the 17th century or Rita Hayworth and Prince Aly Khan in the 1940s; and sometimes to great aplomb - iconic Hollywood beauty Grace Kelly had famously wed Monaco's Prince Ranier in the 1950s. Rumors linking Prince Harry to women in the entertainment industry is also not new, with alleged conquests including TV presenters, actresses, and singers. But the steamy scenes featuring the future royal in black, lacy underwear having a hookup in a legal library in her role as Rachel Zane might give one some pause, just like that fact that Ms. Markle is a divorcee – not unlike the world-shaking and unforgettable Duchess of Windsor, Wallis Simpson, a fellow American who played a major role in the abdication crisis of Edward the VIII in the 1930s. But then again, the Duchess of Cornwall, Camilla Parker Bowles, long-time girlfriend and now-wife of her fiancé's father, Prince Charles, is a divorcee too.

Taken separately, someone who is either of mixed race, an actress or a divorcee seems to have already found a place in a royal family tree. But someone who is all three… well, that is quite new and interesting indeed.

These are just the barest toplines of Meghan Markle's biography– she has not even walked into Prince Charming's sight yet - and there is already so much to know and unpack about this woman, who was suddenly thrust into the international spotlight and inescapably, public scrutiny, in such a short amount of time.

She is such a fascinating public figure, that not only is she among the world's most searched women, she is already the subject of bestselling celebrity biographer Andrew Morton's latest title, Meghan: A Hollywood Princess, slated for release in April 2018. Mr. Morton, it may be recalled, is famous for his New York Times bestseller on no less than Prince Harry's own mother, Diana: Her True Story.

Early excerpts of Mr. Morton's highly-anticipated biography on the latest princess-to-be are already leaving royal watchers clamoring for more information, and the more salacious the details, the better. He isn't the only one willing to spill the beans too; Meghan's paternal half-sister, Samantha Grant, has been making media rounds and peddling her own upcoming book unforgettably titled, The Diary of Princess Pushy's Sister.

People are simply desperate for more Meghan Markle, especially in the days leading up to her May 2018 wedding to Prince Harry. Who is she really, and where did she come from? Is she a social climber and Princess Diana wannabe, as some critics have alleged? Is she really "pushy?" Is she even really "black," as the heated topic of race is unavoidably discussed? What does her extensive humanitarian work and deactivated lifestyle blog, The Tig, have to say about her? How did her first marriage, to one Trevor Engelson, fall apart? How did she and Prince Harry fall in love? What will their wedding be like? What kind of a royal will she be, and how will she fit in with one of the toughest and most beloved families in the world?

Put that Google Search quest on hold, and take a break from sifting through page after page of websites and news clippings. Here, we answer these questions and more, as we take a look at the remarkable life - so far - of Ms. Meghan Markle!

II. #BlackPrincess?

Shortly after the announcement of Prince Harry's engagement to American television actress Meghan Markle, the hashtag #BlackPrincess became viral on the social media platforms Twitter and Instagram, as many African Americans shared their delight in the thought of a person of color joining the royal family. The trending hashtag is just one more feather on the digital cap of Ms. Markle, a successful lifestyle blogger even before she became Google's most searched actor. But the label, while catchy, isn't quite accurate.

When Meghan Markle marries the beloved, red-headed royal rascal Harry (formally known as His Royal Highness Prince Henry of Wales), she will be wife to the man who is in line to the

British throne. Prince Harry trails after his father Charles; older brother William; nephew George and niece Charlotte by William and his wife, Duchess Catherine; and other children they might have. According to royal historians, tradition has it that a male royal receives a title upon his wedding. Prince William and wife Catherine Middleton, for example, were bestowed Duke and Duchess of Cambridge upon their marriage. Similarly, Prince Harry is widely expected to be made a Duke and therefore Meghan, a Duchess. Ms. Markle, in short, is not expected to be called "Princess Meghan."

Title protocols, traditions, and expectations aside, her love story with Prince Harry still refused to shed its fairytale patina, and "#blackprincess" nevertheless became viral, even if it wasn't quite accurate from the "princess" standpoint. The tag's questionable accuracy also stemmed from its more controversial first part, however – that of the actress being "black" to begin with, which has spurred reflection and debate on race and identity in two continents.

Tick a Box / Draw Your Own

The most searched woman on the internet isn't sought on her name alone. The public has shown a marked interest in her ethnicity and many even included the word "black" alongside her name on the search bar. There are plenty of passionate opinion-editorials to find on the subject.

"Reminder: Meghan Markle is Not Black" goes a particularly straightforward article by writer Sandra Rose, citing Ms. Markle's dating history of white men, limited public social interactions with black people beyond her own mother, Doria Ragland, and how observers note that she "doesn't claim us." Cultural commentators, like Elaine Musiwa for Vogue, point out that she is half-black or bi-racial, and expounds on how this is different. And elsewhere, such as in a piece by Nicole Adlman for Hello Giggles, a simple plea – "Can we stop measuring Meghan Markle's blackness?"

Racial identity and relations are complex in most parts of the globe, especially in the politically-charged atmosphere where this cultural moment - the relationship between a popular, white prince and a person of color – is occurring. It may be recalled for example, that early in the couple's relationship, Prince Harry felt compelled to break his usual silence on his personal life by releasing a statement through his Communications Secretary when 'a line was crossed.' Meghan, a girlfriend at the time, "has been subject to a wave of abuse and harassment" through racially-loaded comment pieces and sexist and racist trolling. Ultimately, he feared for her safety and less than two years later, a serious threat would show just how much he had cause to be – a white powder letter with a racist note sent to her in London in February 2018, was intercepted by authorities. The powder, though ultimately ruled harmless, was initially feared to be anthrax. The incident was investigated by the police as a possible racist hate crime.

Meghan Markle has grappled with racial identity issues for far longer than the public has been pondering it about her (or in some cases, using it against her). In a sensitively penned essay for Elle Magazine that has since become one of the most revealing and seminal sources of information about an otherwise private person, she discusses her half-black and half-white parentage and how this has shaped her identity and voice.

Her Caucasian father, Thomas Markle, worked in television as a lighting and photography director. He met her African American mother, Doria Ragland, at a studio in the late-70s. They married, had Meghan, and lived in The Valley in Los Angeles. Meghan shared that their neighborhood lacked in diversity, and how her darker-skinned mother would be mistaken for her, a lighter-skinned baby's, nanny. She had trouble identifying her ethnicity and distinctly remembered leaving the box options blank on a mandatory census asking if she was white, black, Hispanic or Asian. In the acting industry, she was considered "ethnically ambiguous" and found difficulties being cast for a job until she landed the plum role of 'dream girl' Rachel Zane on USA Network's Suits. Ultimately, she would share how she had learned to embrace her mixed-race identity. She 'drew her own box' so to speak, and defined herself - not unlike how her great-great-great grandfather did when the United States abolished slavery in 1865 and former slaves had to choose their own surname.

With her new public role, how Ms. Markle identifies racially may no longer just be about finding herself, however. It isn't just an academic question or intellectual exercise, nor is it just a media talking point or a water cooler topic at the office for the public, either. There could be practical implications. For example, will her inclusion in the royal family affect or re-define British identity, in a highly-charged political atmosphere that has lately "weaponized" race and nationality? Will she, who classifies herself as a humanitarian, use her new position and platform to advocate on racial issues, of which there are several in her new home country? Or will her role as a person of color in a storied institution like the monarchy be largely symbolic? Only time will tell.

Once Upon a Time

Her writing in Elle gave the public a glimpse of a sensitive, intelligent and independent woman looking back at a journey and coming out stronger. But like all self-possessed heroines of legend and fairy tale, her story begins with Once Upon a Time.

Born Rachel Meghan Markle on August 4th, 1981, she was raised in Los Angeles, California by her African-American mother Doria, and British-Dutch-Irish-descent father Thomas.

Doria is a social worker, jewelry maker, and yoga instructor, while Thomas worked as a lighting and photography director for television for several decades. Meghan is their only child together, and after the couple divorced amicably when she was six years old, she lived with her mother.

Her father, who is a Daytime Emmy-award winner, remained involved in much of her life, however. Meghan would recall to Esquire in a 2013 interview that she spent years of her after-school hours on the set of hit 80's sitcom, Married... with Children at his place of work. His other credits include working on General Hospital for 35 years. This exposure would be instrumental in sparking her own interest in the entertainment industry. Thomas was previously married to Roslyn Loveless, with whom he has two children, Meghan's older half-siblings Thomas Jr. and the now-infamous Samantha Grant.

Thomas Sr., now retired, has been described as a bit reclusive lately, and lives quietly in Rosarito, a beach city in Mexico. Despite his physical distance from his Toronto-based daughter, they are said to speak regularly and Meghan has described him, along with her mother, as being very supportive of her. After the engagement announcement, he and Doria released a joint statement through Clarence House, sharing their joy and good wishes for their daughter and her Prince.

Interestingly, "Cinderella" stories aren't so new to the Markles - what with Thomas Sr. reportedly winning $750,000 in the lottery when Meghan was younger. Part of the sum, according to her half-brother Thomas Jr., went to Meghan's private school education. The future royal attended Hollywood Little Red Schoolhouse, and later, all-girl Catholic institution Immaculate Heart High School in Los Angeles.

Markle, who has been described by her half-brother, Thomas Jr., as someone with "laser focus," is not only the first person in her immediate family to graduate from college, she had done so with a double major. She attended Northwestern University in Illinois, having graduated in 2003 with a double major in Theater and International Relations. The self-confessed "theater nerd" was active in her sorority, Kappa Kappa Gamma, and had served in the U.S. Embassy in Argentina during her senior year. One of her professors remembered she had displayed an interest in issues of inclusivity, race and women's rights even then, which are aligned with her current advocacies and humanitarian work.

Her sense of social justice cannot be attributed only to her formal education. Meghan credits her parents, and particularly her mother Doria for raising her "to be a global citizen" aware of the "harsh realities" of the world. Mother and daughter are very close. They are frequently photographed together, and the royal-to-be's mom has also joined her daughter to meet with Prince Harry several times. Meghan speaks often, candidly and highly of the youthful, dreadlocked, free-spirited Doria, who even has a nose ring and can still run a marathon. The clinical therapist/yoga instructor / social worker is involved in the geriatric community and at the Didi Hirsch Mental Health Services in California.

Ms. Markle's family life and her past predictably fell into heavy scrutiny after her romance with Prince Harry became public. Everyone has their own secrets and struggles, but being in the public eye can unearth some embarrassing and painful information.

Among the less positive details media outlets have unearthed and reported about them, are Thomas Sr.'s filing for bankruptcy in 2016, Doria's own filing in 2002, and also that of twice-divorced Thomas Jr., who had also faced gun charges that have since been dropped. He reportedly now works as a window fitter in Oregon. Thomas Jr. has been accommodating to the press, and he is not the only family member who is media-friendly – Meghan's former sister-in-law Tracy Dooley had appeared on Good Morning Britain, alongside Meghan's nephews Thomas and Tyler Dooley. This is to say nothing of Meghan's estranged sister Samantha Grant, who has been openly critical of her.

Samantha, a former actress, and model herself, hasn't let a 2008 multiple sclerosis diagnosis slow her down from a media blitz; aside from writing The Diary of Princess Pushy's Sister, she has been quoted in interviews referring to Meghan as a social climber, and calling Meghan out for not financially supporting their father.

The unconventional set-up and strained relationships is probably why Prince Harry had been quoted as saying his is "the family that I suppose she's never had," a claim that has since been contested by some members of the Markle family.

One would think the royal family Meghan Markle is about to enter shouldn't be too squeamish about tumultuous relationships, as they have well-documented complex histories and entanglements as well as curious characters of their own. But other quarters of the world aren't quite so forgiving. Sometimes, the media in particular can be savage.

"Harry to marry into gangster royalty?" asked Daily Star, referring to Meghan Markle's old neighborhood as rough and known for gang wars. A particularly controversial article on the Daily Mail, "Harry's Girl is (Almost) Straight Outta Compton," has also been widely panned for sharing the family's bankruptcy woes, alongside racial "dog whistles" criticizing where Doria Ragland and even Meghan's aunt, Ava Burrow, live, describing locales as "run-down" and "gang-afflicted" while sharing crime rates and comparing these environments against Prince Harry's and Meghan's ex-husband, Trevor Engelson's, fancier neighborhoods. The latter is rumored to be one of the articles that compelled Prince Harry to break from convention and speak out on his personal life, early into their relationship in 2016.

The unprecedented 2016 statement wouldn't be the only time one or both of the royal couple would have to address the racist undertones and outright attacks levied their way. In their first sit-down interview together for the BBC, Meghan described the situation as "disheartening," and insisted that she was proud of who she is and where she came from.

Unfair attacks aside, what cannot be doubted is that there are strained family relationships to be found in Meghan Markle's past. But that's not the only skeleton in this closet. A video of 18-

year-old Meghan shortly after she graduated from high school, for example, has been circulating the internet. Here, she revealed a strained relationship with her father at the time. While parent-child troubles in the growing up years (Meghan was 36 years old by the time the video came out publicly) can be expected, what is especially jarring is that this video was filmed and unleashed by her former best friend, Ninaki Priddy, a designer in Los Angeles, with whom she had a falling out after an almost lifelong friendship.

Priddy and Markle have known each other since they were two years old and had a close, almost sister-like friendship of thirty years – with intimate photographs to show for it, now also available to the rest of the world thanks to Priddy (and of course, the tabloid industry). Among the photos shared were of the best friends as children, at proms and dances, in school at the Little Red School House and Immaculate Heart High, on road trips and vacations (including one in front of Buckingham Palace!), and at Markle's beach wedding to first husband Trevor Engelson in Jamaica in 2011 – where Priddy had been her maid-of-honor. The bond between the two women ceased shortly after Meghan's divorce, for reasons Priddy has not specifically disclosed outside of saying certain revelations after she met with Engelson ended the friendship. She was no longer in Meghan's life by the time Markle started dating Prince Harry.

III. Meghan Markle: The Working Actress

The Ninaki Priddy video of 18-year-old Meghan Markle was a revelation not only about the royal-to-be's relationship with her father, Thomas, but also about the life and aspirations of a young, aspiring actress. The footage, filmed in 1999, showed the women driving around Los Angeles as Markle prepared for an audition. The role? Dancing in a music video for Latina crossover superstar Shakira, which would have paid her £445 for two days of work. She wouldn't get the part, but as we all know, Meghan Markle's time in the spotlight neither really begins or ends there.

The California girl was exposed to the entertainment industry at a young age, and not just by her geographic proximity to Hollywood. Her father, Thomas, is an award-winning figure in television. Her parents met in a studio, while he worked in lighting and her mother, Doria, was a temp. But the road to Hollywood was not an easy or straightforward one for the actress, who wouldn't find the spotlight until her best-known work as the smart and stunning, legal assistant Rachel Zane in the hit USA Network drama Suits.

Before playing Rachel Zane, Meghan's racially ambiguous features made her difficult to cast in a "label-driven" industry, where color was considered an integral part of character. She tried her best to capitalize on that ambiguity by auditioning for pretty much any role, highlighting whichever ones of her mixed features may be demanded of a character. Still, she found herself languishing in a limbo of not being "black enough" or not being "white enough" for clearly defined, black and white roles.

The stunning actress still managed to rack up a considerable resume, however, with credits on both the big screen and the small screen, starting with a small role as "Nurse Jill" in an episode of General Hospital. She would log in short appearances in hit shows like crime procedurals Castle, CSI: Miami, CSI: New York and Without a Trace; sitcom 'Til Death; CW's remake of 90210; sci-fi drama series Fringe; sports comedy The League; the short-lived, reimagined Knight Rider (where she played a cage fighter!), and as a case model for the game show Deal or No Deal. She would also appear in a collection of lesser-known TV Series and films, many of which were also made for television.

Her big screen appearances pitted her against some big names in show business, albeit in small roles. She sat between Ashton Kutcher and Kal Penn in an airplane in 2005's A Lot Like Love; had appeared as a snarky bartender in the Robert Pattinson (he of iconic Twilight fame) movie, Remember Me; and made a scene-stealing cameo as a beautiful FedEx delivery girl in Horrible Bosses (2011), which starred Jennifer Aniston, Jamie Foxx, Kevin Spacey, Colin Farell, Jason Bateman, Jonathan Sudeikis, Charlie Day and Donald Sutherland.

All in all, her resume reads like that of a quiet, working actor - varied, sometimes random, playing big roles in small projects or small roles in big projects. In interviews, she had talked about her work struggles, and how her parents had helped her make ends meet and pay the bills. She worked a variety of jobs before catching a break, including being a hostess at a restaurant and doing calligraphy. The latter was a part-time job with a memorable and very Hollywood experience; she did calligraphy for the invitations of the wedding between five-time Grammy-nominee Robin Thicke (most famous for the monster hit "Blurred Lines"), and his now ex-wife, film and TV actress, Paula Patton.

It would be her work as Rachel Zane in Suits that would turn the tide away from miscellaneous jobs and small roles and propel her into the spotlight.

Suit Up

Suits is a cable TV drama following the work and personal lives of high-powered lawyers in New York City – particularly, that of superstar closer Harvey Specter and his protégé Mike

Ross, a legal genius and secret college dropout. At a hiring event faced with a set of unimaginative potential recruits, Mike walks in and steals the show, prompting Specter to take a gamble on him despite his lack of credentials. Specter even keeps Mike's fraud a secret from his storied firm, Pearson Hardman. Though initially hiring Mike for his raw talent, Harvey finds a shared passion for winning and eventually, true friendship with Mike. Together, they navigate the shark-infested waters of high powered New York, internal office politics, and romance.

From the very beginning, Meghan Markle was part of the strong ensemble cast of Suits. She played legal assistant and eventual lawyer Rachel Zane, the love interest of the prodigious Mike, from 2011 to 2018. It was a role she could have missed out on. She arrived underdressed for her audition, casually-clad in dark jeans, spaghetti-straps, and heels. To appear more lawyer-like, she popped into an H&M for a $35 little black dress she would later be asked to change into. Another actress, Kim Shaw, was reportedly under consideration for the part as well. Each woman had her own charms. Shaw, a blond, girl-next-door type, would eventually be cast by the same company behind Suits in a dramedy for MTV. Meghan Markle ended up clinching the role of Rachel Zane, and her life would never be the same.

Show creator Aaron Korsh credits Markle's sharp smarts and inextricable sweetness for the close. Then-USA Network executive Jeff Wachtel remarked on her urbane edge and chemistry with boyish star Patrick J. Adams, who starred as Mike Ross.

Mike's romance with Rachel is one of the central storylines in Suits. She is the straight-laced hard worker and him, the flawed but brilliant rule-breaker. Adams described them as a kind of Romeo and Juliet and indeed, over the course of seven seasons, we watch their sexual tension and love heat up and wane amidst legal drama, office politics, and the weight of Mike's secrets.

Suits is a veritable hit with a viewership of over 1.7 million and is now past the 100-episode mark. It is shown and well-loved in many countries and enjoys generally positive critical reviews, with multiple People's Choice Awards nominations and most notably, a Screen Actors Guild Award nomination for Patrick J. Adams. As of this writing, the show has been renewed for an eighth season – but one that would have to be without Meghan Markle, whose departure was announced following her engagement.

The show's flow is not expected to suffer too greatly. Cable TV executive Jeff Wachtel, who had a hand in casting Markle in Suits, remarked that the timing for Rachel Zane's exit was right for a series in its seventh season – a time for change. There may have also been some expectation of these developments anyway, as people on the Suits team had to deal with the complications of having a royal's girlfriend on set; increased security measures, call sheet changes for Meghan's schedule amidst rumors of meeting the Queen, etc. What comes as a larger surprise for fans of the show, however, is that it will return in season 8 without Mike Ross himself, SAG-nominated Patrick J. Adams.

A joint exit, just like Romeo and Juliet, after all - but of course, far less dramatically and far less tragically.

IV. Meghan Markle: Humanitarian, Writer, Editor-in-Chief, Etc., Etc., Etc....

In a 2015 essay for Elle discussing her identity, Meghan Markle describes herself as, among a "mouthful" of other things, an actress, writer, and Editor-in-Chief of The Tig. Prince Harry's wife-to-be is a woman wearing many hats, and bringing Rachel Zane to life on screen is only one of them. She speaks with particular passion about her work as a humanitarian.

In another heartfelt essay, this time for Elle UK, the successful actress is very reflective about her fame and how she reconciles it with the hardships she sees in the world, as well as her role in helping to relieve it. She recognizes the importance of the entertainment industry both as a source of escape for those to consume it and also for herself as a working actress with a platform and a chance – as well as a responsibility – to do greater good. "With fame comes opportunity," she writes, "but it also includes responsibility."

Meghan credits how her parents raised her as a source of her sense of responsibility and social consciousness. What she saw growing up, she claimed, was what she became. Her parents were generous, from giving out spare change to sharing meals at hospices and to the homeless. The scope of her own generosity would range from small actions things to huge ones.

As a teenager she spent days volunteering in Skid Row in Los Angeles; as an actress, she volunteered at a soup kitchen and had arranged with series executives for their extra crew meals be donated there. But her advocacies aren't just about material generosity. They are also about knowledge. She decided her website, The Tig, should "pepper in what matters," with pieces on social consciousness and self-empowerment, aside from its lifestyle content covering fashion, food, travel, and beauty.

Her sense of activism goes back a long way. In a now well-known anecdote about Meghan Markle, she had once written known feminist voices like Hillary Clinton, Gloria Allred and Linda Ellerbee, protesting the tagline of a dishwashing liquid ad that she had found unfair to women. The commercial would later be changed. She was only 11 years old at the time.

The Tig

Meghan Markle's writing is engaging and charismatic, and while her essays have been featured and read in magazines like Elle and Time, her playground is the website of her lifestyle brand, The Tig, launched in 2014 and shut down in April 2017 after about three years of operation. But because this is the Internet Age, nothing goes away quite completely, even if all that one can see left at thetig.com is a sweet farewell ("You've made my days brighter… don't forget your worth…").

Thanks to tools like The Internet Archive's Wayback Machine (said to archive 445 billion web pages chronicling the evolution of the internet), traces of The Tig can still be accessed in the world wide web. These are echoes of the voice and thoughts of the now-ironically more private, but inescapably more public figure behind it. Looking back at a few highlights of the now-defunct website, we get a peek into the mind of Prince Harry's bride-to-be.

Chronicling Moments of Discovery

The Tig draws its name from the shortened mispronunciation of Tignanello, a much-loved red wine with a 600-year history. The "Super-Tuscan" wine comes at a price tag of $90 to $150 a bottle. It's one of Meghan's favorite things, but that is not the only reason she named her website after it. As the first wine that defined characteristics like "body," "legs" and "structure" for her, "Tig" became a metaphor for "getting it" – an ah-ha! moment of discovery. And so her website became a depository of enlightening moments in travel, food, fashion, beauty and other experiences, whether drink-related or not. The ideas, tips, and advice she shared was about how to get more out of life. Some cultural commentators have likened it to Gwyneth Paltrow's Goop (running since 2008), and Blake Lively's Preserve (launched in 2014 and shut down in 2015).

Food and Wine

Given its namesake, there is no surprise that The Tig had a good collection of entries on food and wine. Among them are recipes for both homey dishes and slightly unconventional ones. She shared how-to's for mushroom pasta with creamy truffle sauce, smoked salmon dill dip, beet cheesecake, sweet potato and white bean soup, and, "Combining two of every lady's classic loves," red wine hot chocolate – just to name a few. She also confessed to a love for hot sauce in her food.

Books, Movies, and Music

Cultural commentators have observed that The Tig hints of a fairly grounded celebrity. She showed a liking for cozy, low-key affairs, including morning snuggles with her rescue dogs and intimate affairs with her friends. Like many bloggers, she also had a listing of her beloved books, movies, and music. She used to share her favorite playlists, and her taste in music has been described as eclectic. Among the artists mentioned were Christine And The Queens, Sophie Ellis-Bextor, and Steely Dan.

As for books, she once shared a listing of targeted vacation reads, which included Michael Ondaatje's The English Patient, a love affair set in World War II.

Politics

Ms. Markle's The Tig wasn't afraid of getting personal, while also looking at the big picture.

The actress did not shy away from discussions of race and had even shared her family's experiences. In 2015, a piece called "Champions of Change" honored change-makers like Martin Luther King Jr., Harvey Milk, Gloria Steinem, and, among these iconic names, she also thanked her own parents. Another post, "Because You Must," discussed the imperative for women to vote, along with a history of how the right to do so required the shedding of "blood, sweat, and tears."

Health and Beauty

The Tig also became an outlet for Meghan to share her healthy lifestyle and beauty regimen, from her passion for yoga to her favorite facialists all over the world. And how wouldn't she know about something so specific in various corners of our globe? Her wanderlust and travel chops are also well documented on The Tig.

Travel

Ms. Markle used her website to share her travel experiences, notably one of a month-long, Eat, Pray, Love-type of excursion in Italy. The Tig also featured an impressive collection of insider travel advice on locales from all corners of the world. She and her gaggle of international connections provided comprehensive guides on cities as varied as Athens, Bali, Bordeaux, Madrid, New York, and Paris.

Famous Friends

Meghan's life as it can be glimpsed in The Tig isn't just about having fine things, but also being surrounded by fine relationships. She speaks often and highly of her mother and of hosting her friends. She is also a lover of dogs, specifically her rescue dogs Bogart (a Labrador-Shepherd cross); and Guy (a beagle). Both are now – naturally! – almost as famous as she. Because of her celebrity status, however, it is unavoidable that Ms. Markle's writing peppered with mentions and contributions of impressive friends and acquaintances.

Elettra Wiedermann, daughter of Isabella Rossellini, curated a travel guide for one of Meghan's beloved cities, Paris. Canadian crooner and international superstar Michael Buble had contributed too, with his favorite tracks for the Christmas season. Markle became fast friends with sporting legend and icon, Serena Williams, in 2016, and their friendship is mentioned in the blog.

Life Advice

On the whole, The Tig was about a life well-lived, from material, quantifiable things to less measurable things like extraordinary experiences and even improving your outlook. She had entries on improving positivity, and advice on self-love and fostering independence. Among her most interesting tips? Going to movies alone and treating oneself out to dinner!

From Refugee Camps to Red Carpets

The Tig has been shut down since April 2017, and Meghan Markle's social media accounts would follow not long afterward in early 2018, in keeping with her status as a future member of the British royal family. This is not unexpected because, though some members of the monarchy do have official accounts, these are maintained by their respective households and are comparatively impersonal in terms of content. Kensington Palace's communications team are expected to post for her after their wedding – as is the case for Prince William and his wife, Duchess Catherine.

It's a lot of platform to lose; at the end of 2017, Meghan's Instagram following clocked in at almost 2 million, while her Twitter account has crossed the 350,000 mark. But with the deactivation of The Tig and her other social media presence, Ms. Markle could hardly be described as silenced.

Her voice has only been getting bolder and louder over time, as she championed a multitude of causes. She is an advocate for UN Women, and her work there has brought her into the sphere of both women in power, and those who need their voices heard.

In Kigali, Rwanda, for example, she met with both female parliamentarians and grass-roots leaders at a refugee camp. As an advocate for the organization, she has also graced the stage for a powerful speech on International Women's Day, courting a standing ovation from UN Secretary-General Ban Ki-moon himself – one of her heroes. He, along with politicians and diplomats like Madeline Albright, are the kind of people she looks up to and considers as celebrities.

Meghan Markle would be making her way to Rwanda several times. Aside from going there for UN Women, she also stopped over in her work as a global ambassador for World Vision, looking at projects in providing access to clean water. Her tasks for World Vision also included travel to Delhi and Mumbai in India, to advocate for menstrual health. She would write about her experience in Time Magazine, linking access to feminine products as a contributing factor in women's potential.

Meghan Markle has also been active as a Counsellor with One Young World, an organization that brings together young leaders from all over the world. In this role, she has shared the stage with the likes of Canada's media savvy Prime Minister, Justin Trudeau.

Anyone can get whiplash, having to navigate the extremes of having so much in her life as a successful television actress, and the lack of basic necessities she sees in her charitable works. She had described the dissonance as a swinging pendulum. But from what she has shown the world, she is able to navigate Hollywood and humanitarianism with aplomb.

As she had mentioned on her website, she shifts between refugee camps and red carpets.

Now, she adds another "R-" a new responsibility, a new cap to wear, and another side to her already multi-faceted life – Royalty.

V. When Harry Met Meghan

Here's another twist on how this modern-day Cinderella story is not like the well-worn fairytales of old. A short search can demystify the titular queen of all mystery girls, yes, but let it not be forgotten that in Meghan and Harry's tale, "Prince Charming" has his own interesting backstory. To begin with, he has a name. The name - Windsor.

And what a complex history it carries.

Diana's Son

His Royal Highness Prince Henry of Wales was born in London, England on the 15th of September, 1984. He is the second son to Charles, Prince of Wales, and Princess Diana, formerly Lady Diana Spencer, daughter of Earl Spencer. There is no discussion of Prince Harry without an understanding of his complex upbringing.

The blond and blue-eyed Diana was a stunningly beautiful English rose, but she wouldn't leave a legacy of being "The People's Princess" based on these legendary looks alone. She had already moved in the circles of the royal family since childhood, but she wouldn't be catapulted into the limelight until her courtship and eventual marriage to the reserved heir to the British throne, Prince Charles, who was 13 years older.

They married on the 29th of July, 1981, in a ceremony broadcast the world over that would eventually be dubbed, "Wedding of the Century." Prince Charles and Princess Diana would have two sons – William Arthur Philip Louis, born in 1982; and "Harry" himself, Henry Charles Albert David in 1984.

Prince Harry's parents, unfortunately, would not have a happily-ever-after together. Their years of marriage would be known for difficulties, including issues of infidelity as well as Princess Diana's depression and bulimia. The couple's separation was announced in 1992, and their divorce was finalized in 1996. Charles would eventually go on to marry longtime, on-and-off flame and controversial figure, Camilla Parker Bowles, in 2005. Diana's life after her royal marriage, on the other hand, took a tragic turn much earlier on. She died in a 1997 car crash while evading intrusive paparazzi in Paris. Also dead were her boyfriend, Egyptian film producer, Dodi Fayed, and their driver.

The world was shocked by Diana's sudden death. She remained a public figure and was beloved all over the world for her beauty and humanitarian work even after she and Prince Charles divorced. During her lifetime, she was associated with at least 100 charities. The world mourned her loss, and felt special sympathy for her two handsome sons, William and Harry (then aged 15 and 12 years respectively), especially when they bravely joined their mother's funeral procession. Millions of people tuned into the funeral ceremony and procession, just as they did during the events of Diana's life as a royal, just as they did for her wedding to Prince Charles.

The same blinding glare of the spotlights and camera flashes would follow her sons and those they loved for the rest of their own lives.

The Bad Boy Party Prince

All young people make mistakes as they grow older, but for someone like Prince Harry who's got the eye of the world on his every move, these mistakes can make it to the front of tabloids all over the world. There are many reasons why Prince Harry has been called "iconoclastic" and "royal rogue" in the press, among them:

Admitting to underage drinking and smoking marijuana in 2002; getting into a scuffle with paparazzi outside a London club in 2004; being accused of cheating at the storied Eton, an all-boys boarding school; wearing a Nazi-themed outfit to a "Colonial and Native" costume party in 2005; using a racially insensitive term on a fellow soldier who was of Pakistani-descent in 2006; accused of animal cruelty in 2010 during a polo match; and unforgettably, getting photographed naked in 2012, after a game of strip billiards in Las Vegas.

What would follow these misadventures are spectacular spreads on tabloids and other media, and cycles of criticism, staid official statements and public apologies, before the next misstep – and all the above incidents is to say nothing of the string of women linked to the Prince during his time as one of the world's most eligible bachelors.

Still, it wasn't all fun and games for Prince Harry. Like his late mother and his father, Prince Charles, he was heavily involved in charity work and had other, very serious pursuits. In May 2005, he enrolled at Sandhurst and would eventually join the Household Cavalry. He served in Afghanistan in 2008.

Afterward, he trained as a helicopter pilot with the Army Air Corps and did a second tour of duty in Afghanistan in 2012.

After ten years of service with the British Army, he ended his military career in 2015 to focus on charity work and his duties as a Prince, but the military was never far from his mind or heart – being a champion for the cause of wounded soldiers is one of his most prominent and cherished roles. Indeed, his and Ms. Meghan Markle's public debut as a couple was in Toronto in 2017, at the Invictus Games – an international sporting contest for injured, wounded and sick, serving or veteran servicemen and women – that he launched in 2014.

Everyone loves the image of a reformed rake, but the truth is, Prince Harry has been heavily involved in many works of charity for a long time now. He set up Sentebale in Africa with Prince Seeiso all the way back in 2006, in honor of their mothers. The charity focuses on the needs of children from Botswana and Lesotho, who are in extreme poverty and affected by HIV/AIDS. Princess Diana, it may be recalled, was one of the most influential advocates for those suffering from the disease in the 1980s- a time when so much misinformation, fear, and shame was attached to it. Prince Harry would continue this legacy by working with the Terrence Higgins Trust. The very modern and tech-savvy royal would also take an HIV test live on social media platform Facebook, to normalize HIV testing and to show that it can be easy to do. He would also take a public test in Barbados with superstar Rihanna on World AIDS Day 2016. Prince Harry is also a patron of

WellChild, a charity for sick kids, and had recently founded the Heads Together campaign alongside the Duke and Duchess of Cambridge. Heads Together aims to foster better, more open discussions on mental health, as well as raise funds for mental health services. It may be recalled that Prince Harry's mother, Princess Diana, had publicly admitted to mental health issues during an interview with journalist Martin Bashir in 1995.

Prince Harry paints a picture of a global citizen with social consciousness, even from his position of privilege and fame. In this sense, it seems almost destined that he would meet and fall in love with someone like actress and humanitarian, Meghan Markle.

The Road to You

But before there was Meghan, the world's most eligible royal had romantic entanglements aplenty – both rumored and real.

In 2003, Prince Harry was linked to TV presenter Natalie Pinkham, who has since married and had two children. Shortly afterward, in 2004, he met model Cassie Sumner at a London nightclub. It would reportedly be the last of their scandalous encounters. This short meeting would leave a lasting impression though, thanks to a racy account shared by Ms. Sumner, which included details on touching and flirting.

Zimbabwean national, Chelsy Davy, would capture the Prince's attention for a far lengthier period of time - much longer than even his relationship with Meghan Markle before he eventually proposed to her. Prince Harry and

Ms. Davy became an item during the gap year he spent in Africa, and they dated on and off from 2004 to 2011. He had even brought her to his brother's wedding in 2011. Though the romance didn't bring them down the aisle, it has since been revealed that they remained friendly.

Prince Harry had shorter rumored romances in these unsteady relationship years – with hit show X-Factor host Caroline Flack; and Norwegian singer Camila Romestrand. The entertainment industry continued to prove a romantic lure for the redheaded royal indeed, as his latter love interests were also in the fields of fashion, movies, television, and music. He was linked to posh actress/model Florence Brudenell-Bruce in 2011, now married to multi-millionaire Henry St. George. He reportedly dated another well-heeled actress, fellow aristocrat Cressida Bonas (said to have been introduced to him by his cousin Princess Eugenie), from 2012 to 2014; Mollie King of girl group The Saturdays was a brief interest in 2012; and he had reportedly cozied up to pop star Ellie Goulding in 2016. He has been acquainted with the singer for years now – she performed at his brother's wedding in 2011 and for the Invictus Games in 2014.

Prince Harry's eventual Cinderella, Meghan Markle, has a considerable, rumored and real romantic history herself. Canadian chef Cory Vitiello, a lifestyle TV figure and successful restaurateur, was in the picture from 2014 to 2016. She was briefly linked to golfing superstar Rory McIlroy before that, though there was never any confirmation of a relationship between the two. The most notable of her past romances was with American film producer

Trevor Engelson, whom she was with from 2004 to 2013. Engelson's film credits include Remember me, License to Wed, All About Steve, and a few television projects, including Snowfall and a Heathers remake.

While Meghan's dating past presents a much shorter list than Prince Harry's, it is her deep and lengthy romance with Engelson that had her critics' eyebrows rising. They met when she was just a little over a year out of college on a night out in Los Angeles, and the pair were together for around seven years, engaged in 2010 and married in 2011. The marriage ended in a no-fault divorce in 2013, for irreconcilable differences.

Speculations abound on the reasons for the collapse of the marriage, with rumors swirling left and right from both named and unnamed sources. Some have claimed the end came out of nowhere, while others say fame may have changed Meghan after several successful seasons of Suits. Other say the long-distance relationship – she was based in Canada for the television show she starred in, while he ran an office in Los Angeles – was a contributing factor. The parties themselves remain mum on the subject.

A Whirlwind Romance

Prince Harry dates an actress… it could have been any headline on any paper about most of the beautiful women abovementioned since the public took interest in the royal's personal life in his late-teenage years. But in July 2016, he was set up on a blind date with Suits actress Meghan Markle and neither of their lives would ever be the same.

The Prince and Meghan were set up by a female mutual friend, whose identity they kept secret to honor her privacy. Though this theory is yet to be confirmed, some royal watchers and amateur sleuths speculate the friend might have been fashion designer Misha Nonoo. She straddles the lines between fashion, entertainment, and royalty on two continents. She was previously in a romance with Alexander Gilkes, a friend to the Princes William and Harry, and also enjoys connections with Princess Eugenie on top of having the skills and networks to be able to dress stylish stars like Emma Watson, Cate Blanchett, and Meghan Markle. Interestingly, Meghan would wear a white, button-down Misha Nonoo shirt called 'Husband' to her and Harry's public debut as a couple at the Invictus Games in 2017.

Another possibility is one Violet von Westenholz, who has long moved in royal circles and also became friendly with Markle while working in P.R. for Ralph Lauren. No further information is forthcoming from the royal couple or any of the "accused," however, and the identity of their matchmaker is still a mystery.

Regardless of who may have set up the royal couple, sparks flew right away. In a candid interview with the BBC, Prince Harry described himself as "beautifully surprised" when he saw her and that he knew he had to 'up his game.' He must have been on point, as he and Markle would go on two consecutive dates in London. A few weeks after that, in August, they went on a five-day vacation in Botswana, a quiet country in southern Africa boasting a low population density and a lot of protected land devoted to the wilderness. There, they really got to know each other; they had limited direct knowledge of the other person prior to dating, even though they were both in the public eye. Prince Harry had not seen Suits nor heard of Meghan Markle before, while she did not grow up in the tabloid culture that has hounded him and his family. Thus, while holidaying together in Botswana, their love blossomed under a blanket of stars, in the middle of the relatively untamed wilderness.

It is a country and continent close to the Prince's heart; it was a place of refuge after his mother's untimely death, and ever since then has become a place where he can relax and be himself. He has returned repeatedly for his charities and wildlife conservation work, as well as - if some sources are to be believed – romancing several other women prior to Ms. Markle. After all, who wouldn't be impressed by stunning views and magnificent wildlife in the ultimate glamping date?

Their quiet romance wouldn't remain so for long. The irrepressible tabloids were quick to catch on a good story, and by October of that year, reports were already circulating on the couple's relationship. Prince Harry and Meghan Markle stayed mum on the subject until an unprecedented November 2016 statement from Kensington Palace on behalf of the Prince was released. In it, the romance was confirmed amid condemnation of how Ms. Markle had been represented by some media outlets, and how was being harassed by trolls. The statement referred to Meghan as the Prince's girlfriend – a distinction that would be even clearer come December of that same year when photographs finally emerged of the elusive couple. Papers published photos of the Prince and Ms. Markle out and about in London.

The New Year brought even more romantic milestones. Reports circulated of Meghan meeting Harry's sister-in-law, the Duchess of Cambridge in January 2017, and in March, they attended a friend's wedding in Jamaica. The Tig, Meghan's lifestyle brand and website, says farewell shortly afterward, in April. In the following month, she attended the wedding reception of the Duchess of Cambridge's sister, Pippa Middleton, as Prince Harry's date. May 2017 may have also been the month that the Prince sought his grandmother, the Queen Elizabeth's permission to marry Meghan.

The couple returned to Africa and August, stirring up a fury of engagement rumors. But no announcement was made soon after, even with an eventful September – Markle appeared on the cover of Vanity Fair proclaiming their love, and they appeared together officially at the Invictus Games held in Toronto.

November of 2017 was monumental too – The month saw Meghan leaving her hit show and moving to Kensington Palace. They announced their engagement on the 27th and held a photo shoot at the Sunken Gardens of Kensington Palace. On the 28th, it was announced that the marriage was set for May 2018, at St. George's Chapel, Windsor Castle, and that the Royals would be footing the bill.

VI. Another "Wedding of the Century"

As of this writing, the upcoming wedding between Prince Harry is still a month away but royal fever is already in high gear, with details on the big day emerging little by little. One thing's for sure though – it would be a relief for anyone that it's a royal family paying for this extravaganza!

The Proposal and That Ring!

The wedding is sure to be a spectacle for the millions expected to witness it on television screens all over the world. In high contrast, the low-key couple were engaged quietly at Kensington Palace during a cozy evening while preparing a meal. They would recall the sweet proposal during an interview with the BBC, sharing how the Prince romantically got down on one knee and how "she didn't even let me finish."

The stunning ring placed on her finger by the Prince is said to have been designed by Harry himself. It features a center stone from Botswana in memory of their magical time there together, flanked by two side stones from Princess Diana's collection – a sweet gesture in honor of the beloved mother who remained a constant influence in the Prince's life. The stones rest on a yellow gold band.

Meghan's upcoming wedding band is expected to carry some history too; by royal tradition, Welsh mines have been the source of gold for royal wedding bands since 1923, when the Queen's parents, King George VI and Elizabeth Bowes-Lyon, married. It would be the same for the Queen and Prince Philip in 1947, and for Prince William and Kate Middleton in 2011.

The Wedding Dress

Meghan Markle's lifestyle brand The Tig chronicled the eye-opening discoveries of a well-lived life. This beautiful woman is a connoisseur and a tastemaker, and many are eager to find out how her sense of style will translate to a wedding fit for a royal – especially when it comes to the dress.

Photos of Meghan Markle in a wedding dress are easy to find. In character as Rachel Zane for her hit show Suits, she was beautiful in a deep V-neck, A-line gown by Anne Barge. Images are also available from her first marriage to Trevor Engelson in 2011. They held festivities before 100 guests in Jamaica, with a traditional Jewish chair dance and beach games and barbecues. The bride was outfitted in a bohemian-style, strapless sheath dress adorned with a jeweled belt. It was very boho chic and indeed, she would later share a taste for simple styles and subtlety, counting Carolyn Bessette Kennedy's iconic Narciso Rodriguez dress as among her favorites.

For her wedding to Prince Harry, royal watchers are expecting a departure from the beach look and hoping for Couture and tasteful style risks – which she had displayed a flair for in her official engagement photos with Prince Harry, wearing a sheer black, $80,000 stunner by Ralph & Russo. Bets are on for the fashion house that would win the coup of dressing the next royal bride. Names that have been bandied around include Ralph & Russo; Duchess Kate's beloved McQueen; and Meghan Markle's friend Roland Mouret. This is expected to be a well-kept secret until we see Ms. Markle garbed for her walk down the aisle.

The Ceremony

The Ceremony will be held at noon, at St. George's Chapel in Windsor Castle. Prince Harry was christened here. It has been reported that The Dean of Windsor, The Rt Reverend David Conner, will be in charge of the service while the Archbishop of Canterbury, Justin Welby, will be the officiant during the wedding vows. He also officiated the recent baptism and confirmation of Meghan Markle into the Church of England, in a ceremony held privately at the Chapel Royal in St. James' Palace.

Their marriage vows will be followed by a romantic and oh-so-royal carriage procession, in a route that was designed to give more people a chance to see the couple and share in their special day.

Not everyone can have a prince for a groom or a carriage procession, but everyone knows a romantic day in celebration of love wouldn't be complete without flowers. The Royals turned to Philippa Craddock for floral arrangements at St. George's Chapel and St. George's Hall. She is expected to work with florists from the Chapel as well as Buckingham Palace, using locally-sourced, seasonal flora like foxgloves, peonies and white garden roses.

The Reception(s!)

Meghan Markle is a lover of food and fine living but either way, dining and especially the wedding cake, is expected to be the very best in any royal wedding.

600 people are expected at the chapel for the ceremony and the luncheon reception at Windsor Castle, hosted by the groom's grandmother, Queen Elizabeth. A private sit-down dinner for 200 will later be held at Frogmore House, this one to be hosted by Prince Harry's father, Charles.

To celebrate their love this season of Spring, the Royals turned to confectioner Claire Ptak of London's Violet Bakery. It has been announced that a season-appropriate wedding cake of lemon and elderflower will be covered in buttercream and styled with fresh blooms.

The Crowds

A royal wedding is always a magical experience, and a show of force from the military always adds that extra oomph. The Ministry of Defense announced participation from various services of the armed forces – The Windsor Castle Guard, Household Cavalry, Navy, Marines, Air Corps, RAF and Royal Ghurka Rifles will be on hand, with music from the Band of the Irish Guards as well as State Trumpeteers. They will be lining the streets of the venue, participating in parades and making music, as if the royals and their guests weren't a spectacle all on their own!

A lucky 2,640 exemplary members of the public will have an intimate view of this historic event – they were welcomed to share the royal wedding experience by giving them access to the grounds of Windsor Castle. What a view!

The Guest List and Invitations

So who are these guests that spectators can look forward to seeing?

There are really still so many unknowns about the wedding, even as it is only just a few weeks away, and the mystery (and controversy!) surrounding the guest list and wedding party are among the biggest ones.

Of Meghan's family, it is not known if anyone has been invited aside from her divorced parents, the very private Thomas Markle Sr., and Meghan's beloved mother Doria Ragland. It is also not known if either or both of them are walking her down the aisle. There have also been no announcements on a Bridesmaid squad, though some of Meghan's famous friends would surely make the wedding even more of a show – she has close relationships with beautiful Quantico star Priyanka Chopra, tennis legend Serena Williams, and Canadian stylist Jessica Mulroney. Famous faces from the entertainment industry are expected to be in attendance, especially from Meghan's hit show Suits and from Prince Harry's own showbiz connections. Rumors are, a couple of the Prince's ex-girlfriends with whom he remained friends, may also be on the guest list.

The Best Man role is also yet to be confirmed, with speculation falling on Harry's older brother William, or perhaps one of Harry's close friends. Prince William's picture-perfect family is expected to have some participation too, however – he and Duchess Kate's children, Prince George and Prince Charlotte, have already logged some wedding party credentials under their belts, having previously been on their Aunt Pippa Middleton's entourage. Their third sibling, whom the Duchess is due to give birth to in April, is not expected to make an appearance.

There are political and diplomatic considerations to be had, too. The royal couple are good friends with former United States President Barack Obama, and there was early speculation that he and wife, former First Lady Michelle would be invited. That would not be the case, however, and his exclusion from the guest list, as well as that of his successor, President Donald Trump as well as that of the UK's own Prime Minister Theresa May, makes the event seem staunchly apolitical.

As for those lucky enough to get an invitation… it may be recalled that Ms. Markle reportedly supplemented her income when she was a struggling actress with calligraphy, such as what she had done for the wedding invitations of hitmaker Robin Thicke and his (now) ex-wife, actress Paula Patton. Ms. Markle therefore probably has a good eye for elegant writing on a good piece of paper.

The extent of her involvement in the invitations to her own wedding is not known at this time, but the white English cardstock invitations, with elegant gold and black American ink in cursive, is highly formal and steeped in tradition. It features the badge of the Prince of Wales and was made by London-based Barnard & Westwood, the workshop behind royal invites since the mid-1980s.

It would be a dream come true for many a royal watcher to get such an invitation, but in the meantime, as more and more details are revealed on the approach to the special day, most people will just have to wait and see and eventually watch from afar, as one of history's

most favorite, reformed royal rogues marries
his Cinderella.

VII. Conclusion: Meghan Markle's Second Act

Meghan Markle's relationship to Prince Harry changed everything in her life. Some of these changes started to happen even before they were officially engaged, with only more to come afterward. She had to say goodbye to acting. Passion projects like The Tig and platforms on social media that she had spent years of effort to build and nurture had to be shuttered. Immediately following their engagement announcement, she was shuttled to event after event after event, in duties and responsibilities as a royal-to-be.

It can be overwhelming for anyone to be so deeply caught in the public eye. History would tell us this kind of lifestyle can be exhausting and even damaging to even the hardiest of minds and bodies. The initial wave of harassment and abuse that Meghan Markle had to face early in her relationship to the Prince, even just as the latest romantic interest in a long list, was but a glimpse of the kind of scrutiny she would have to deal with. Once she is officially within the royal family, the stakes would only be higher. Inevitably, she will be compared to the widely adored Duchess Kate, Prince William's wife, and the People's Princess herself, Harry's mother, Diana.

Already, some quarters are calling Ms. Markle a Princess Diana wannabe, a kind of "Princess Diana 2.0." But so far, how she will shape her own legacy is still largely unknown. She isn't a new version of Princess Diana, she is barely even Meghan Markle as she is best recognized –

the biracial, divorcee, television actress and lifestyle blogger.

She is at the cusp of a new iteration.

Here, just before her wedding to Prince Harry and the beginning of a new life, we are all at the Intermission. Act One is done; she has quit her day job. She will find a new version of herself that can thrive in the old world of a legendary monarchy, with its enduring structures and rigid rules. Things are about to get bigger and brighter and splashier. We are entering Meghan Markle's Second Act, and what she has in store for the world, we do not yet know.

What we do know, however, is that she is a determined woman with a particular vision for the world she lives in. From her own powerful words in an essay penned for Elle UK: fame comes with opportunities and responsibilities, and "to focus less on glass slippers and more on pushing through glass ceilings."

Now that's for a modern-day Cinderella!

Kate Middleton

The Commoner Who Would Be Queen

Michael Woodford

Introduction

In the lead up to the 20th anniversary of his mother's death, Prince Harry – brother in law to Kate Middleton – made some interesting observations about the monarchy.

He firstly said that the younger generation of royals feels that it is their role to modernize the monarchy.

In so doing, these royals believe, they will maintain its popularity and sustain its role for doing good.

They consider that, by bringing the House of Windsor into line with 21st century thinking, attitudes and lifestyles, they will enhance their own standing.

But not for selfish purposes, or for self-aggrandizement. No, for far more altruistic reasons.

They feel that from a position of trust and popularity they can do more to support charities, help the poor and suffering and improve the world.

These are noble aims, and are to be applauded.

But Harry said another thing in the interview.

In extending the idea of duty and responsibility to Great Britain, to the Commonwealth and, where possible, the world he recognized that one day one of the young royals would be monarch themselves.

It was just that, none of them wanted to do it.

They knew that they would have to, but just as hoovering the sitting room or putting out the bins has to be done but is not much fun, it is a necessary but unappealing job.

We can wonder whether this thought was anywhere in the mind of Kate Middleton, Berkshire lass, when she agreed to marry Prince William? And one day become his queen.

We might also consider how much she thought about the fact that everything she chose to do would be scrutinized, analysed and, often, criticized.

An Education

Tradition and heritage are important concepts to the Royal Family. After all, the line can be traced back far into history.

It was therefore understandable that Prince William should choose the third oldest educational institution in the English speaking world for his alma mater.

The University of St Andrews sits on the coast in the picturesque region of Fife, Scotland.   The oldest of the four main universities in the country, it was the place where Kate and William met.

Rather in fitting with his mother's wish for her boys to see real life, St Andrews (as it is known) has one of the most diverse student bodies in the United Kingdom.

It is also a highly regarded institution, ranking only behind Oxford and Cambridge in terms of academic prowess.

Founded in 1410, it is home to a fraction over 10000 students. The town itself is only a little bigger in terms of population.

It was the seat of learning to a number of well-known personalities including, in recent times, politicians Alex Salmond and Michael Fallon.

Olympic champion cyclist Christ Hoy also attended the university. As did, joining in 2001, a certain couple who would soon dominate the pages of newspapers and magazines.

As well as the rapidly expanding fields of on line news and gossip.

They were not alone in discovering romance at the University – 1 in 10 students find their life partner there, a case of love and learning combining.

The old town stands just 60 miles to the north of Edinburgh in the quietest corner of Fife. So maybe there is little else to do but fall in love?

Certainly, the stunning landscapes, with sandy beaches and magnificent sea views, are the stuff of romantic novels.

The excellent restaurants, few, but of high quality, lend themselves to candlelit dinners and quiet chat over a glass of fine wine.

Perhaps they provide the answer to the University's success in matchmaking?

Or, of course, the famous St Andrew's golf links, home to events including the Open Championship.

The 'old course' is one of eleven in the immediate area. Its traditional old hotel would become a favorite haunt of the dating couple.

Before her death, Princess Diana (along with Prince Charles), had secured a degree of privacy from the media for their sons.

Here they could get to know their peers, and establish friendships which would, as many do for university students, endure.

Sallies (St Salvator's Hall) looks like the stuff of dreams. Honeyed brick work and ivy clad walls, the coast just a short walk away. It is a destination in itself.

The phrase 'accommodation block' would be like calling Balmoral the country cottage.

Kate and William would undoubtedly have bumped into each other during their first year even had they had little in common. In fact, they shared many interests.

Sallies accommodates only 276 students, which includes its more modern annex, Gannochy House.

If the exterior of Sallies is wonderful, internally it is even more magnificent.

Although constructed relatively recently, (the 1930s), the enormous, oak beamed dining hall and stained-glass windows suggest more the baronial home of a Shakespearean Thane than student digs.

In fitting with a residence chosen by a royal, Sallies runs things in a very traditional way.

High Table operates once a week, when students are invited to join lecturers and other dignitaries for dinner. One suspects that this honor may have been extended to the future king.

Overlooking the edifice that is St Andrew's Castle, Sallies is a warmly welcoming place for its young inhabitants.

And if that description sounds like it has come from an upmarket holiday brochure, then fair enough. St Andrews and Sallies really are special places.

Kate's room was a couple of floors above William's, and the two often used to meet at the same time for breakfast. They soon discovered shared interests and traits.

Both were shy – William even considered pulling out of University - and by Christmas had become good friends. They shared a love of sport, and regularly went jogging and swimming together.

As often as Kate and William might have chatted on a jog, dined on the same table, or moaned about a particular assignment, it was in 2002 that the first seeds of a stronger relationship were sown.

A charity fashion event was taking place in the famous five-star hotel, Fairmont St Andrews, which was close to the university.

Kate was modelling at the event, and strode down the catwalk wearing a knitted dress.

The see-through garment was later sold for £78000.

Prince William was captivated. However, the meeting may never have happened.

Prior to gaining a place at St Andrews, Kate had in fact applied to another Scottish University, Edinburgh.

Quite late in the day, she changed her mind, although there was no certainty that she would get a place at the highly popular St Andrews.

Some think that it was a chance event that led her to actually seek to follow the future King to his university. But this is unlikely.

However, some pupils from Marlborough (Kate's school) and Eton (William's place of learning) happened to meet up while both were still at school.

Parties involving the affluent children at boarding schools often take place in holiday times.

The friends are frequently spread around the country, so guests can come from far and wide.

Although both were at this particular gathering, along with the younger Prince Harry, there is no certainty that the two even spoke to each other.

Back in Scotland, following the seminal charity fashion show, the two (not yet a couple) decided to flat share for their second year at University.

Along with friends Fergus Boyd and Olivia Bleasdale, they rented a flat in a fine terrace in the town.

Although somewhat smaller than the homes they had grown up in, the building oozes traditional Scottish charm, with its long sash windows, ornate chimney stack and solid brick build.

Boyd, who drew William's attention to Kate at the charity show by whispering 'Wow, Kate's hot!' is an old Etonian friend of the Prince and was later made Godfather to Prince George.

Olivia Bleasdale also remained close friends with the couple, and was invited to their wedding.

However, the four were lucky to get the flat at all. Charlotte Smith, the landlady, had imposed a 'girls only' policy on letting the property.

She had rented it to a group of boys some years before, and they had left it in a state. Her worry was that, off the leash from their boarding school upbringing and year in halls, William and Fergus might let rip.

The girls had discovered the home, and when they raised the idea of sharing it with two boys, in a purely platonic sense, Smith had initially said no.

It was then revealed that one of the men was Prince William. Even at that point, Smith was unsure and decided to discuss it with her husband.

But, if you can't trust a prince, who can you trust? They talked it through with neighbors. After all, a member of the royal family comes with more baggage than just his cases.

But the neighbors were happy, and they agreed to let the flat. Apparently, the four students were ideal tenants, and did not even complain about the rent.

Mind you, we can reasonably assume it was well within their means to pay.

Kate was described by her landlady as very caring. Indeed, the whole group came across as a very nice collection of young adults.

It was during their time in the flat that Kate and William's friendship grew even closer, just beginning to edge into the romance that would lead to marriage.

If St Andrews as a town did not offer a huge range of entertainment, what it had was of good quality.

A favorite haunt was the Jahingir Indian restaurant. It was quite new back then, and a picture of its royal customer hangs in the curry house.

Today, a student special costs £9.95 and a Balti is available for under £12. Slightly different from the banquets the couple now attends.

Although the only electricity between the two still seemed to be the latent static from the thunderstorms rolling in off the North Sea, they did attend each other's 21st birthday bashes.

But then, one would expect no different of flatmates.

It was during their second year in the flat, and the third at St Andrews, that the friendship blossomed further. Christmas 2003 was the point that friends believed mutual love had burst through.

Their relationship was officially confirmed three months later, on April 1st 2004. Pictures of them skiing together at Klosters leaked out from paparrazi spies and the relationship had to be announced.

The couple then moved out of the flat for their final year, sharing a cottage on the edge of the town.

With their finals approaching (both would eventually graduate with 2:1s) work began to take precedence over romance but the two were again seen at Klosters, and at the 56th birthday for William's father.

The event at Highgrove for Charles was a relatively private affair.

After university, William demonstrated his mother's attitude of wanting more from life than just that of a working royal by deciding to follow a career in the military.

Whilst it was always traditional for male royals to follow this route, in his case, it was a genuine career choice.

However, things were tougher for Kate. She was and was not a part of the royal set up.

Whilst she had the down side of the press interest in everything she did, she did not yet get the level of protection and screening that her boyfriend enjoyed.

A bit part job in the clothing chain, Jigsaw (which was owned by a family friend) was followed by returning to work in her parents' business, Party Pieces. In the mean-time, she waited. And waited.

William's career was taking off – literally, he would become a flying officer – but Kate was caught between her own life and the pressures of being associated with the second in line to the throne.

When William enrolled into Sandhurst, the officers' training ground, they knew that opportunities for time together would be limited during the year long course.

Following his training, William was commissioned and became an officer in the Blues and Royals (following his younger brother, who did not attend university).

Pressure was mounting on the couple, and at an event at Cheltenham racecourse, they seemed cold towards each other.

Revelations then followed that William had been seen dancing with another woman at a nightclub.

The couple had shared a cooling off period during their final year at university, but had got back together quickly.

This time, with the two more mature, the problems seemed deeper. Kate, though, took the opportunity to enjoy herself.

Dressing up, partying and generally having a good time. Going out with her sister,

Pippa. She began to find much needed breathing space.

And, as the saying goes, absence made the heart grow fonder. Three months later, the two were once more a couple.

Even better for getting away from the incessant attention, they set up home on island of Anglesey, where William's work as a search and rescue pilot took them.

The pair rented a four-bedroomed whitewashed cottage in the Welsh speaking hamlet of Bordorgan, which is in the south west of the tiny island.

The owner, George Meyrick, was well known to royals, and used to invite the couple into his own home, a stately pile, for shepherd's pie and claret.

Having been spoiled by the scenery in Scotland, they found the views from Anglesey just as spectacular. Their farmhouse overlooked a small beach and was wonderfully isolated.

Although the location was meant to be kept secret, for security reasons, it was widely known on the island and because a tourist attraction for visitors, albeit an unofficial one.

The couple settled comfortably and, almost certainly, with relief into the quiet community.

And there was clearly something in the fresh Welsh air, because just four months after they arrived, William proposed and Kate accepted.

They holidayed in Kenya (where William actually popped the question) but back in Wales, although their home was isolated, they were on friendly terms with locals when they saw them.

They would often stop for a chat. Kate liked to shop in Homebased, buying cute items for their home (no antique furnishings with historical associations then).

William would leave for work - his security team in close attendance – regularly at a quarter to seven. Occasionally, his work helicopter would collect him.

Kate would shop, buying fish for dinner and trawling the local Waitrose, protection officer trying to blend seamlessly into the background.

There were no heirs and graces, the couple dressing casually and committing to their new home environment.

Visits to the cinema and surfing would occupy their leisure time. Occasionally, the young couple would return to the follies of their student days.

On one occasion they dressed up in silly wigs and costumes in order to get incognito into the cinema. Unfortunately, in staid Anglesey, they stood out even more than normal.

Another attempt at disguise saw them riding around in a white van, and motor biking through the scenic country lanes was another past time.

When they finally left Anglesey – by this time married – it was with great sadness. Sadness to themselves and the locals.

By this time William's posting was over, but the residents say that they are always welcome to return.

As for the cottage, that was not put back onto the market. But, rather like the flat in

Hope Terrace, St Andrews, it was left in immaculate order.

Even the gym equipment that filled one of the bedrooms left no marks. It was an astonishingly ordinary spell of time for the future wife of the King of England and wonderful for that.

If locals were treated kindly, others had a harder time.

A sky TV repairman had arrived on the island to sort something for the Rupert Murdoch owned company.

But, and we have all been here, his Sat Nav took him to the wrong place. Driving down a winding track, he was suddenly pounced up by black suited protection officers.

He must have thought he had been transported to one of the American action movies his employer so often broadcast.

'You look incredible Beautiful'

April 29th, 2011 - The date of the wedding of Kate Middleton to Prince William.

Thirty years previously, when his parents had married, the superlative claims had seemed justified.

'Marriage made in heaven' and 'fairy tale marriage' were not just hyperbole, but the genuine belief of a nation who saw royalty as different and rather special.

We know more these days, and as splendid as the occasion was, there was no intention of setting the couple up for a fall.

But with the economy in freefall thanks largely to the Arab spring, and Syria entering civil war, the world needed something to lift their spirits.

And when it comes to pomp, splendor and tradition, nobody quite does it like the British.

Two billion people tuned in for the wedding, a brief glimpse of the sun in a cloudy world.

Kate had kept the details of her dress secret. Designed by Sarah Burton as a part of the Alexander McQueen fashion dynasty, the ivory and lace dress set off her looks to perfection.

As well, it enthralled the fashion industry, causing more fizz than an over shaken bottle of bubbly.

Her ring, which was a tight fit and a struggle to put on - the only moment of anxiety during the ceremony - was of classic Welsh gold, and had been given to the Prince by his grandmother.

It was very much a British occasion.

Nineteen hundred guests crowded into Westminster Abbey, with hundreds of thousands outside. It went without a hitch.

From the 1902 royal landau which took the couple from the ceremony, to the lunchtime reception hosted by the Queen, the event had to be perfect, and it was.

Kate wore a diamond encrusted tiara, lent by the Queen, which gave her the appearance of a Princess.

But by making her grandson Duke of Cambridge, the Queen had made Kate a duchess. Perhaps there were too many bad historical memories left in the term 'Princess'.

During the ceremony itself, a prayer – written by the now Royal couple – was read out. Otherwise, the service was un-notable.

Afterwards, the journey amongst the throngs passed through Parliament Square, beyond

Whitehall and onto Horse Guards Parade. It was cheered at every trot.

Down the Mall and into the Palace went the couple, waving and smiling, and onto the Reception hosted by the Queen.

Crowds had been queuing for hours – days in some cases – to get the best views and they were rewarded at 1.30, when they saw what they had come for.

Kate and William appeared on the Buckingham Palace balcony and kissed before the cheering masses.

A fly past followed, with a World War Two Lancaster bomber guarded by two spitfires rumbling over the Palace to cheers and roars.

Tornado and Typhoon jets followed. The newly appointed Duke, pointing out the planes to his smiling wife, offered a second kiss.

A clear sense prevailed that this was a chance to celebrate and show off the nation, its present and its past.

As much as she must have been expecting the enormous reaction, Kate (now Duchess of Cambridge) was seen to murmur 'Oh my' as she saw the cheering public.

The day finished more privately, with the Prince of Wales hosting a private dinner for close friends and family.

It had been a mixture of the pomp and privacy that the royals manage with great skill.

Motherhood

The newer generations of royals are fulfilling their aim and their duty as they see it, to address the challenges and problems facing us all.

Included amongst these for young parents, mothers especially, are mental health issues.

Kate admits that, even with the levels of support to which she has access, being a mother is really difficult.

As she says, despite all the advice you can get (wanted, or otherwise) a lot of the time you just make it up as you go along.

This is especially true as she coped with two pre-school aged children. This sense of not being sure that your decisions are right, or if you should be handling matters differently, can really impact on a mum.

It can lead to feelings of loneliness and inadequacy, leading on to full scale depression.

By talking about such mental health concerns, and showing that a duchess is as susceptible to them as anybody, Kate hopes to demystify these previously hidden illnesses.

By bring them into the open; she hopes that people will feel more confident talking about their feelings, their worries. Thus, they will be more willing to get help.

Of course, her children's grandmother, Diana, suffered enormously from depression through William's early years, only revealing publicly her problems shortly before her death.

Kate and William have two children. George was born on 22nd July 2013, with his sister Charlotte joining the world on May 2nd 2015.

Her pregnancy with George was not an easy one, and resulted in an earlier than usual public announcement.

She had been admitted to hospital and, of course, the press had a field day spreading rumor and promoting assumption.

The couple felt it better to announce the pregnancy, and reveal that the hospital attendance was to cope with extreme morning sickness, than to let the rumors continue apace.

It would be nice to say that the Duchess's second pregnancy was easier, but the unborn Charlotte caused as much nausea as her brother.

Had they been born the other way round, with Charlotte appearing first, then the birth would have made history.

Following centuries of male primogeniture (male children surpassing their older sisters in the order of heirdom to the throne), the

Government had decided to move the royals forward a century or ten.

It is now the first born who becomes heir, irrespective of whether this is a boy or a girl.

George will soon be starting his formal education; his parents have chosen one of the independent St Thomas's schools in London.

This fits very much with William's own upbringing. Diana, with Charles agreeing, forewent the tradition of using private tutors for their children's early years.

This was in line with the young princes gaining as normal a childhood as possible, using the tube and visiting London Zoo.

Given that William and Kate are seeking to modernize the monarchy, it seems likely that their children will follow a route that many other children of wealthy parents take.

So what are the possible educational paths of George, Charlotte and any other children the couple might have?

Despite the wish to give their children as normal an upbringing as possible, it seems highly unlikely that they would completely break with tradition and use state schools.

That might just be a step too far.

The Thomas's group of schools, to which George is enrolled, takes children up to the age of 13 in two of their branches.

Thomas' are day schools, and commutable from the couple's Kensington Palace home. However, even William and his brother Harry attended boarding schools from a young age.

Whether the children will do the same will be one of the first key decisions the parents have to make.

If the children follow in the footsteps of recent generations and develop a passion for sport and the outdoors, then a move out of London might be on the cards.

That would mean one of three things: the whole family moves, but this could cause problems with the growing state duties that Kate and William incur.

Secondly, the young children could commute. Increasing numbers of youngsters do this. There is a huge growth in the number of Prep Schools just outside the M25 who offer a mixture of boarding and day facilities.

Possibly 'flexi-boarding' could be the answer, giving the children more time at home but also an introduction to boarding. This would, to a degree, satisfy tradition.

Finally, of course, the children could follow the traditional route of joining a full boarding prep school.

The last option opens up William's old place of learning, Ludgrove (in Wokingham) as a possibility. The school certainly is secluded, which makes security easier to handle.

But only for George, as it is an all-boys school.

Cheam, where Prince Charles and George's great uncles went, is another possibility. With a strong reputation for care, and a location just outside Newbury, it is close enough for him to get home for weekends off.

Mind you, these 'exeat' breaks are only occasional through the term, lessons and sport usually taking place on a Saturday.

There is a further question for our modernizing royals to consider. Should their children attend single sex or co-educational schools?

There are plenty of both from which to choose. Perhaps an option such as St George's Windsor might fit the bill.

The school has a royal heritage – Princess Beatrice is a past pupil – and its attachment to Windsor Castle means that Great Granny and Grandad might look after the kids.

The same question remains for the senior school, which usually begins at 13 for those educated privately.

Day Schools in London, such as St Paul's and City of London offer single sex day education.

Or maybe they will follow in their parents' footsteps. Eton for George and Marlborough for Charlotte.

Whatever the choices might be, we can be fairly sure that the young royals have their names on a waiting list already. And they are unlikely to be turned down.

Another consideration is that the very traditional schools that Princes Charles, and older generations, attended either no longer exist, or have changed out of all recognition.

He described Gordonstoun as 'Colditz in Kilts'; the school is far more welcoming today. Eton is no longer just a bastion of wealth and privilege (although plenty of that remains).

Rather, it is a multi-cultural school which, through its extensive bursaries, takes boys from a variety of backgrounds. It is often at the forefront of educational ideas.

Whereas at Prince Charles' Prep School, Hill House, marching formed a part of the curriculum until recently. (Apparently, something to do with insufficient rooms for the pupils.)

Times have changed.

So, whatever option has been chosen, Kate and William's children will get a taste of something akin to normal life.

At least, normal for one born into wealth and opportunity.

In another break from tradition, but one which echoes William's upbringing under Princess Diana's influence, the young children have already participated in an overseas tour.

George was just three and his sister still toddling when they accompanied their parents on an official visit to Canada.

Of course, the reaction from the Canadian public at seeing the youngsters was ecstatic.

Diana had taken William to Australia on tour when he was a baby, but only after a huge battle with the palace, who felt he should be looked after by nannies.

The children have also been page boy and bridesmaid at their Aunt's wedding. The youngsters stole the show at Pippa Middleton's event.

Mind you, George had a bit of a tantrum during the long drawn out service, getting himself told off by his mum. It's reassuring that even royal children have their moments.

Perhaps he was following in his father's footsteps? William was only a little older when he went to his Uncle Andrew's wedding.

At that event he pulled faces, looked extremely cross and was reluctant to hold hands with his fellow assistant. To be fair, though, that was a girl! (His cousin, Laura Fellowes).

Growing Up

Kate, or Catherine as she is actually named, is not a typical bride for a future king. Although from a very comfortable middle-class family, she is not connected to the royalty.

That makes her an unusual, but not unheard of, choice.

Her father's family had distant ties to the aristocracy, which gave access to some trust funds. These helped financially when she was younger.

Her parents originally worked in the aviation industry. Her father was a flight despatcher and her mother a flight attendant.

Later, they set up a highly successful business, which is now worth tens of millions of pounds.

Catherine (her name was shortened to Kate only when she moved to University) was christened in Bradfield, Berkshire after her Reading birth.

This was on January 9th 1982. It is highly unlikely that her midwife would have suspected how famous the new born would become.

Bradfield is a delightful little village, dominated by the boarding college of the same name. Indeed, this whole area of England, full of rolling hills, green fields and south of the Thames is delightful.

And rather well off.

Working for British Airways, the family was posted to Jordan, in the Middle East, when Kate was just two.

The family spent two years there, and Kate attended an English speaking nursery.

On their return to England, the family moved to Chapel Row, a tiny hamlet near Bucklebury, which lies just to the south of the M4 and east of Newbury.

From there, she joined St Andrews Prep School in Pangbourne.

The school shares some characteristics with her future husband's Prep, Ludgrove. Both are set rurally, near small towns.

Each caters for the children of the wealthy, and is traditional in its outlook.

Both are accessed down a long drive, making them seem more remote from the real world than they actually are.

St Andrews is, though, co-educational and, unlike the all-boys Ludgrove, has optional rather than compulsory boarding.

Kate's family took advantage of this, and she was mostly a day pupil who boarded with increasing regularity when she was older.

Separated by under twenty miles it is more than likely that the future couple would have inadvertently met, if not spoken, at some school event of other.

Perhaps a time when Ludgrove boys visited the school for a fixture, maybe for a musical event or theatre experience.

Kate was, like the family she would join, interested in sports. She was a fine athlete, and held the school high jump record for a number of years.

She left St Andrews when 13, and moved to Downe House near Newbury. Unfortunately, the change of school did not work out for her.

The girls' only atmosphere allied with the fact that she was a naturally shy person meant that she found it hard to fit in.

Quite quickly, she became a target for bullying. Indeed, the impact of the two terms that she spent at Downe House in the mid-1990s may have come out later.

At her wedding, she requested that the guests make contributions to, amongst others, an anti-bullying charity. This in place of the superfluous need for normal gifts.

The then Head teacher, Susan Cameron, preferred the term 'teasing' to bullying. But whatever, the culprits and indeed the facts of the events have remained secret.

Sporty pupils like Kate often get on well with their peers, but equally girls in their early teens can be thoughtless in their comments.

Miss Cameron told a British newspaper that she thought Kate was unhappy and unsettled, but not the recipient of serious bullying.

But, victims would say that bullying is bullying. The action of singling out one child or a group of children, for continued nastiness is deeply upsetting to the victims.

That Kate remained at her Prep School until the end, whereas girl only schools often transfer their pupils at 11, meant that friendship groups were already established.

This may also have made the settling in period more challenging than normal.

In addition, Kate was an especially strong hockey player, but had little experience of playing the school's main sport, lacrosse.

For somebody who had been top of her tree at prep school to suddenly move down the pecking order can be hard. Especially when there is unpleasantness – no, let us avoid euphemism - bullying around.

Downe House features a number of well-known alumni, including sports presenter Clare Balding, comedy actress Mirandha Hart and model Sophie Dahl.

But Kate used to cry herself to sleep there. However, Miss Cameron's take on the experience is interesting.

She believed that it helped turn Kate into the strong lady that she is today. Others might see longer term effects of bullying, or teasing if you prefer, as more negative.

In fact, as extremely harmful, the notion that it is character building is quite outdated.

However, Kate managed to secure a place at Marlborough School.   Here, life was much better for her, and echoed more her time at St Andrews.

She was known still as being quiet, but was hard working, popular and extremely sporty. She was also quite down to earth, and became one of the crowd.

Past pupils include the singer Chris De Burgh, poets John Betjeman and Siegfried Sassoon and Sally Bercow, wife of the Speaker of the House of Commons.

The spy Anthony Blunt also attended Marlborough.

Rather like William's extremely old-fashioned attire at Eton, Marlborough includes oddities amongst its uniform, including a long black skirt.

However, in the full boarding community, there was, and remains, a mix of backgrounds.

Parties in stately homes, polo and other evidence of the privilege of wealth are common, but so are the children whose parents scraped together the fees (now over £30000 per annum) and lived a relatively austere life as a result.

Kate did well at the school and her results put her in a position to choose the university that appealed most to her.

She gained excellent grades in her A level subjects, which were Chemistry and Biology, along with Art.

However, before higher education, like many teenagers with the backing and independence to do so, she took a gap year.

In effect, this was two gap 'half years', combining time in Italy with a trip to Patagonia.

The gap year would be a chance to de-stress after her A levels and gain some life experiences that she could draw upon as she got older.

Given the direction her life would take, this might well have proved to be a good decision.

She began the year with an intensive twelve week course at the British Institute in the beautiful Italian city of Florence.

This would give her a chance to develop her love of art, learning about the great works in the city. Also, she would be able to explore the culture of this, one of the world's great destinations.

Following Florence, she decided to take on a physically and emotionally much tougher challenge. She would participate in an Operation Raleigh working visit to Chile.

Although she did not know it at the time, her decision was an omen towards the direction her life was soon to take.

Prince William had been on the same excursion just weeks before. He had loved the experience, and, had Kate simply swapped the order of her gap year experiences, they could well have met then.

Her group consisted of 150 young people from all walks of life, with many being wealthy young men and women who had also recently finished their A levels at boarding school.

But the party also included teenagers from more normal backgrounds as well as young offenders who were given the opportunity to use the experience to get their lives back on track.

Those who had recently been in drug rehabilitation programs were also on the trip.

Climatic conditions in Patagonia would be, at the time of year they travelled (British winter), similar to a British Autumn. Lingering warmth would be countered by a lot of rain.

Kate took work on the boat, BT Global Challenge, where her duties included everything from chatting with guests to cleaning and helping with deck duties such as lowering the ship's sails.

After that, she developed her knowledge with work in the field of science. She assisted on projects collecting organisms and analyzing sea life for conservation purposes.

She was seen, rather as in her school days, as a hardworking, strong and athletic person who got on with her duties willingly and without any fuss.

She seemed determined to get the absolute most out of her experience.

Another skill that Kate was beginning to exhibit was her ability to relate to children. She was successful in helping out in a local school, teaching English.

Kate had grown into a very beautiful young lady, who got on well with boys as well as girls. But, according to the leaders of the trip, she was never of the slightest trouble to them.

After they were married, Kate and William were able to thank the Operation Raleigh staff and volunteers in a small way. They met a group at a project in Borneo.

From her gap year, Kate moved on to University. Her original choice had been to study History of Art at Edinburgh, but, of course, she swapped, completing her education at St Andrews.

Various claims have been made that this was so that she could be at the same venue as

Prince William, whose choice was announced before she changed her mind.

However, many students alter their destination, and the appeals of both St Andrews and Edinburgh are considerable, if different.

Edinburgh University is set in the heart of the city, at the center of a large cultural and financial hotspot.

Whilst its view down the Royal Mile to the Firth of Forth is, on a sunny day, of great magnificence, the city is more renowned for its architecture.

Edinburgh is a great university, but its reputation for art is not as high as that of St

Andrews. And, it has over three times as many students as the Fife institution.

For a quiet girl, who had grown up in countryside settings and who had spent much of her gap year developing her love of her subject, to swap was not such an odd choice to make.

Miners, Kings and Party Pieces

Kate was five when her mum realized that she had a difficulty that could well be shared by many others in the country.

With two very young children, plus another on the way, and living in an affluent area, birthday parties were a bit of a problem. And, in particular, what to put in the bags at the end of the day.

Sweets and tat were the only real options beyond a slice of birthday cake.

Inspiration was provided for the Middleton family business, Party Pieces. From humble beginnings in the garden shed, the company took off big time.

As it expanded, Kate's father Michael gave up his job as a flight despatcher and joined in, then more and more employees. The business outgrew its shed and moved a nearby farm.

Selling balloons, bunting, cakes, confetti and almost anything else you can imagine connected with parties, the business certainly benefitted from Kate's royal connections.

Visits to its website increased by over 160% in the week the couple's wedding was announced, and having a link to the House of Windsor definitely helped with credibility.

Carole Middleton, Kate's mother, is undoubtedly a driven person. Whether as an entrepreneur or in supporting her children, she is a conspicuous figure.

She grew up in more humble surroundings than she now enjoys and attended her local state schools.

Tracing back far enough, and with enough convenient marriages and leaps of faith, her lineage can be tracked to Edward IV, who was King of England in the 15th Century.

But that her great grandfather was a Durham miner is a better indication that Carole is very much not of blue blooded heritage.

Now, however, her heritage is reflected on the golden chevron on the coat of arms given to the couple. Her maiden name is Goldsmith.

Her nature is such that from time to time press coverage of Carole Middleton has been less than flattering.

Stories that she has driven Kate into various decisions to manipulate her relationship with William and the royals abound.

She has been accused of encouraging Kate to disregard royal traditions by having a significant say in the procedures she follows.

Included amongst these are the arrangements around her bodyguard, and whether it should be a man or woman.

She was accused of being behind Kate's decision to change universities to be with William at St Andrews.

Currently, she is apparently encouraging Kate, whose two pregnancies so far have been difficult, to have another child.

There have been many other stories, linking alleged problems in the royal marriage back to Carole and making miles out of meters regarding royal treats, such as access to the royal box at Wimbledon.

Allegations of poor relations with the House of Windsor are manifold in the tabloids and on-line gossip sites. And so on.

But there are many counter points to be considered. Firstly, in the age in which we live, there is in no reason why a husband's family should have a greater input into a marriage than a wife's.

It wouldn't happen in a marriage where the husband is not a prince, so there is no reason why it should when he is one.

Secondly, most of the stories are without much basis, relying on rumor and unsubstantiated leaks. On top of this, we all know that the media loves a bit of gossip.

Thirdly, there is absolutely no reason why Kate, who has a strong relationship with her mother, should not call on her for advice and guidance.

After all, the record of the royals with regards to William's mother is unimpressive, although things have changed. Carole has made a more than decent job with her own three children.

The younger royals talk frequently about modernizing the monarchy, making it truer to real life. Letting a young mother seek advice from her own mum is an example of them doing this.

If Carole's link to any royal heritage is so tenuous as to have no real substance, then her husband's link to aristocracy is a little closer – although still pretty distant.

However, the connections did mean that he grew up comfortably, with trust funds providing income for the family.

He has a direct link to King Edward III, who ruled in the thirteen hundreds, but closer, his grandmother – Olive – was an aristocrat.

Unlike his wife, Michael did attend an independent school, Clifton College in Bristol.

Kate has two siblings, Pippa and James, the latter followed her to Marlborough whilst Pippa went to Downe House, where her more outgoing personality meant that she had a much happier time than her sister.

Of the two, Pippa is more regularly in the news.

Classified as a 'socialite', she married in 2017. She is also a columnist and author. And has, like her sister, worked in the family business.

James is an entrepreneur who has created more than one company. He is active in raising awareness about his learning difficulty, dyslexia.

A Much-Maligned Duchess

An awful lot of people are happy to offer their views on Kate Middleton.

This probably results from mixture of her position and that (relatively speaking) she has come from a standing of ordinariness to royalty, inspiring just a dusting of jealousy.

 Also, people's willingness to cast views and aspersions on who they wish is just how things are in latter part of the 2010s.

Social media means that many hold a view on everything, and (seemingly) it doesn't matter how we express it.

The result is a see saw of positive and negative reports and comments.

Perhaps it is the Diana effect, but the public feels that they have the right to know everything a royal does.

At the same time, not all views expressed about Kate are negative, far from it.

And she is influential. Just by becoming wife of a future king, she was described by Time Magazine as one of the planet's most significant people.

Perhaps being the first royal wife to hold a university degree is a part of that.

But this positive note is countered by the negativity displayed around her wearing 25 outfits on a week-long tour to Canada.

Is that really such an excessive amount for a nine-day visit?

She is clearly an icon for fashion, just like Diana before her; a dress she wore generated such interest that they sold at a rate of one a minute after she was photographed in it.

But signing a pre-nuptial agreement is seen as bad. She is presented as 'one of us' shopping in Waitrose and Tescos, buying ingredients for the cooking she loves to do.

But her parenting skills are scrutinized by the public and in the press.

This up and down relationship with the public is reflected in, or maybe led by, her relationship with the media.

Certainly, she can become frustrated with photo sessions and lengthy media occasions. But sometimes coverage of her has gone too far.

From the early days, post university, it has been a love hate relationship. A part of the problem might be that Kate and William are considered celebrities as much as royals.

And that means, in the eyes of many, that they are open to as much scrutiny as anybody chooses to give them.

With so many platforms on which to broadcast 'news', a never ending supply is needed.

If that dries up, it is seen as legitimate to speculate and hypothesise in a negative way. Hence the unevidenced guesswork into the royal couple's parenting skills.

There have been specific events which have undermined Kate's trust in the media. In 2012, a French magazine printed grainy photographs, taken from a huge distance, of her sunbathing topless on a beach.

Something completely normal for the setting in which it occurred.

Even more disturbing, given heightened security fears over terrorist actions around the world, two paparazzi recently followed Prince George when he was playing in the park with his nanny.

The sense is there that the royals cannot win – criticized if they put up the covers and are viewed as distant from the populace, but exploited when they do appear, informally, in public.

If Kate can become angry at the intrusion into private matters by the press, then her husband is even more determined to keep them a minimum.

He considers legal action appropriate for unwanted and unwarranted intrusion. Of course, he experienced the suffering his mother went through at the invasive nature of the media.

In addition, he will have in his thinking the skiing holiday in Klosters in 2005.

At this event, his father had forgotten that he was wired up, and broadcast his views about the BBC correspondent, Nicholas Witchell – an 'awful' man, according to Charles' comment.

And a Daily Mail journalist wormed her way into the young royals' party set, only to reveal all to the nation.

Perhaps unsurprisingly, the press is not welcome on their holidays.

Kate, too, has won damages for their unceasing intrusions.

However, the media see it differently. They feel that the royal couple needs to understand that the public are interested in them, and as such they should allow more access.

British papers become frustrated as they largely fall in line with the requests of the palace but see their overseas colleagues publishing freely abroad.

Certainly, viewing footage of the pressure put on Kate before her marriage is disturbing.

Hordes of paparazzi chase her down the street, sometimes on motorcycles, and flash photography explodes in her face. At times she is almost pushed to the ground such is the mindless desire for a close up.

It does not engender good relationships. Comments from senior journalists along the lines that the public 'need to know', and the only way to prove a story is to get the photo, seems self-serving.

It has created the situation where royals of William and Kate's generation are seeking to take control of their own media stories.

Kate used The Huffington Post, an online blogging news site, to promote her relationship with a mental health charity.

At the same time royal correspondents, flavor of the month so recently at the Queen's Jubilee celebrations, now fear for their jobs.

They suspect that social media will become the main platform for royal stories in the future. Of course, in a way, that is a return to the old days of the public just being told 'what is good for them'.

At the same time, many of the paparazzi can only blame themselves for the situation.

Trusted photographers are permitted at private events. But many of the photographs released of the royal children are taken by Kate herself, and distributed via social media.

Shock, horror. After all, it is unheard of for mums to proudly publish photographs of their children on social sites! Especially if they are, as is Kate, keen amateur photographers.

The press speaks cynically of 'Middleton Rules', the conditions created by William and Kate's father around what might or might not be published.

But then this might be a reasonable response to being called 'work-shy' and the 'invisible princess' by some British papers.

It seems as though the press want it both ways. They urge the royals to be more normal, more accessible, but then exploit the freedom this gains.

They seem to forget that in the pre-Diana days, whilst the royal correspondents might have been more accepted, the stories they were offered were stage managed.

And the press seems to have lost track of the fact that times have moved on.

Whilst they might need photos of a smiling Prince George to sell papers, the Cambridge family does not need the press to share their message.

The world is changing.

Although, of course, the press might not agree.

Royal Relationships

The Queen warmed quickly to her grandson's girlfriend and that relationship has stayed strong throughout the couple's subsequent marriage.

She is, naturally enough, particularly fond of the two great grandchildren, George and Charlotte, and leaves gifts for them when she visits.

However, despite the generally positive feelings the two shows for each other, there have been times when matters between Kate and her monarch have become strained.

The Queen is, of course, renowned for her work ethic and her belief in duty above all.

When Kate was struggling with her health during her pregnancies, bad feeling did bubble up.

Kate had a particularly severe form of morning sickness, and anybody who has experienced this knows how debilitating it can be.

It resulted in her missing a number of public events and whilst there was sympathy from the head of the household at the outset, the Queen did feel that enough was enough.

That Kate should get out of her sickbed and return to complete her engagements. William, though, was worried that a too early return to work could have longer term health implications.

There was also a small dispute over George's first birthday party. The Queen offered the formal setting of Balmoral but Kate chose instead to hold the event in their London apartment.

She felt that the youngster would have more fun at home.

Even though niggles such as this might from time to time arise, it is very little different from many homes where an elderly matriarch cannot quite come to terms with how the young ones behave.

Another area of concern between the two is also generational. The Queen from time to time expresses doubts over Kate's choice of dress.

Whilst many would disagree over the older royal's views, Kate is seen as a style icon. Her style receives endless coverage especially when stretching royal protocol.

On occasion, her clothes have been regarded as too revealing for the position she holds.

But despite these odd disagreements, Kate describes the Queen as a calming, gentle and wise influence in her life, and that of her children.

The relationship Kate has with her father in law and Camilla Parker Bowles is also generally strong with occasional moments of conflict.

Inevitably, frictions that do occur tend to be over the grand children, and have focused more on the role played by Kate's parents than the couple themselves.

However, Kate and William have worked hard to ensure that there are equal opportunities for all the grandparents to play their part.

It is, though, extremely difficult to avoid the pernickety criticisms seen in the press when every aspect of their lives is scrutinized.

One of the royals with whom Kate shares a laugh is Prince Phillip.

Although she and William do not always attend the usual royal celebrations at

Sandringham (don't most couples share around the Christmases?) the elderly Phillip is well known for his, admittedly un-PC, and sense of humor.

William holds a close tie with his brother Harry, and Kate too is fond of her younger brother in law.

The pair shares a sense of humor, and Harry is particularly good with his niece and nephew.

Living close to his brother and sister in law, they often meet, sharing a meal or a session watching Game of Thrones.

Kate also provides a sisterly influence in his life, and has been a great advisor over

Harry's romance with the actress Meghan Markle.

In particular, she has passed on her experiences of coping with the media attention.

When pictured together, usually with William making up the three, Harry and Kate exhibit a clear warmth and friendship. Kate looks more relaxed than when in more formal situations.

The three have also worked together on charities, most notably recently launching the Heads Together mental health organization with which the two brothers have strong personal ties.

Another royal with whom Kate gets on particularly well is the Countess of Wessex, Sophie.

The two share their 'commoner' backgrounds, and also a love of shopping. They are often seen at Wimbledon in each other's company.

Zara Tindall's love of sports draws her close with both Kate and William. She is George's Godmother, and at royal gatherings they will usually gravitate together.

Perhaps two of the royals with whom there is less of a natural bond are Princesses Beatrice and Eugenie.

However, there are no problems between the children of Prince Andrew and Kate, more that they share less in common.

The challenge of joining a family such as the Windsors is that they are more than just a family. They are an institution and one that is in the public eye.

Meeting the family is difficult for any outsider, and Kate seems to have made a decent fist of it. Inevitably, and very typically, there will have been some tensions.

But these are normal, it is just that for most they are not scrutinized and shared by outsiders.

Similarly, Kate's parents are often criticized as though, because they are commoners, they somehow have less to offer.

And less right to be involved. In fact, William, Harry and their generation have stressed their wish to continue the work their mother, inadvertently, began.

Now the princes are old enough to make a difference, they have gone about the modernization process which is essential for the good of the monarchy.

Kate has played her part, in often very difficult circumstances, in all of this.

Troubled Times

It is interesting to scan through some of the online gossip – nonsense might be a better word – that emerges around Kate and William's marriage.

One unnamed site uses two vastly different and unrelated quotes to form an article which more or less declares the marriage over.

On the one hand is unsubstantiated rumor that Kate was pregnant with her third child, but had not announced it (at the time of the article, she decidedly was not pregnant).

This is then linked to a comment overheard by a teenager who saw Prince William on a tour to New Zealand.

Asked how many children he would like, he smilingly says 'Two'. He is hardly likely to say another number, given the headlines that would cause.

The teenager reports this back to the media. Such is the basis for the fact that the couple are in marital trouble. Kate is pregnant with child number 3 (she isn't) and William doesn't want it (there's nothing to want).

With a rare sense of self scrutiny, this particular outlet realizes that the story is, to put it mildly, thin. So, to back up the point, reference is made to their up and down times during courtship.

And to seal the deal, it manages to twist that fact that the couple is seen together in public, apparently deeply fond of each other and having a good time, as further proof of a break up.

Clearly, the article claims, being seen jointly in public only occurs to dampen down rumors of a split. Apparently, the Queen has 'ordered' the two to appear together.

Against this type of over-hyped nonsense, it is impossible to draw accurate conclusions. It would be a strange marriage if there were not, from time to time, disagreements.

But let us try to look at the facts. It was widely reported that Kate moved out of London and back with her parents whilst she was pregnant with Charlotte.

This was assumed, in some quarters, to be evidence of a separation.

That depends on how you interpret the word. In the most literal sense, William and his wife were separate for a spell. Just as they are if he undertakes royal duties alone.

We know that Kate was extremely ill during her pregnancy. We know that their London home is a hotbed of media interest. We can guess that, when faced with extreme nausea, you want to be away from all of that.

And we can safely deduce that you also want to be with loved ones. Where are most wives likely to head in those circumstances? To their mum, this is where Kate stayed.

Returning to the article, it ends by asking the readers to offer their views as to whether the marriage is on the rocks.

It is a strange society where the uninformed opinions of those unrelated to the topic form the basis of what makes news.

The article in questions was followed, a short while later, by another piece which stated that social media was buzzing with the news that the couple were going to get divorced.

Well, it must be true then.

Another story claims that the Queen has forced the couple apart, calling them work shy and insisting on greater commitment to royal duties.

Ummm. A likely series of events.

When it was announced that her son, Charles, and Princess Diana were separating, she was so upset (even though she knew the announcement was coming) that she took her corgis for a walk.

She returned to Sandringham, where she was staying at the time, turned around and took them out again for another long stroll.

She then repeated the activity. Such was her upset that she needed to be alone to get her head around the announcement. Lucky corgis.

We do know that William and Kate had some breaks during their courtship. As we saw earlier, these were in the lead up to their finals at University, then when William was away with army duties.

In both cases, they found that they wanted to be together again.

Of course, there may have been problems earlier in their marriage. There may be problems today. One day, we might find out from a reliable source.

We did with Charles and Diana, when Diana revealed the truth firstly to the author

Andrew Morton and later in a BBC documentary.

But, even more probably, their marriage is strong.

And if it is not, is it really any of our business?

Doing Her Duty - and more

In line with other royals, Kate is patron and supporter of many charities. Her association with Heads Up, the mental health support organization, is one of her newer ones.

William and Harry are also involved. Their personal experiences of bereavement and the associated mental health concerns following their mother's death provoking such commitment.

Another organization which is particularly dear to Kate is Beatbullying. She suffered herself as a young teen, and now seeks to do all she can to help others in this very difficult position.

Since the birth of her children, she has also become an active advocate of opposition to cyber bullying.

She and her husband met with heads of Facebook and Twitter to discuss ways in which this insidious behavior can be tackled.

One of the unique horrors of cyber bullying is that it is ubiquitous. Like it or not, young people are hooked onto social media, chat rooms and the like.

A bully can exploit this by sending a message at any time. The impact of the fear of the ping on a victim's phone or laptop has led, in severe cases, to suicide.

Bereavement as a child is, naturally, a cause close to William's heart. He is patron of Child Bereavement UK, and Kate supports him actively in his work.

She has talked with and offered sympathy to both adult members who have lost their own children, and youngsters who are suffering bereavement.

She is also a patron of EACH (East Anglia's Children's Hospices). Kate and William lived in Norfolk before returning to London, and the region is close to her heart.

With EACH, she visits and supports children directly as they face their final days.

Two other of the many charities she supports reflect her own love of art. She is patron of the National Portrait Gallery and Art Room.

The latter combines her desire to support those who are most vulnerable with her passion for art. The charity seeks to address issues around self-esteem and teaches life skills to vulnerable children.

It looks to use the power of art to make children more confident and better able to fit into their world. Art Room works with kids who have become disengaged, often excluded, from school.

Indeed, her willingness to give her time to the most vulnerable, and therefore most neglected, members of society is one of her strengths.

She is patron to Action on Addiction. This charity works with drug and alcohol dependents, working to help them to break free from their condition.

Increasingly, with the seemingly unregulated (to any significant degree) rise of online gambling sites, the charity also seeks to support those caught up in this destructive problem.

She is also a supporter of M-PACT, which is unique in being an organization that works with the families of alcohol and substance abusers, seeking to bring them together.

Amongst the numerous other charities which have her patronage, large and small, are The Anna Freud Centre, the 1851 Trust, Action for Children and Sportsaid.

When it comes to charity work, Kate certainly pulls her weight.

Despite the movements forward it has made in the last twenty to thirty years, and these have been considerable, the monarchy remains a somewhat staid and pompous institution.

That is not to suggest that the family is like this. And in all likelihood some of the officials associated with the running of the Palace are not complete fuddy duddies.

(It must be remembered that it was not that long ago that Andrew Morton's book about Diana, written with her direct input, led to the kind of reactionary response that ought to make people laugh.

Amongst other claims and accusations, Morton was called a traitor, and told that he should be imprisoned in the Tower of London.)

But perhaps it is one of the joys of the monarchy that it does still employ outdated and over grand pretensions. This is, after all, what attracts the tourists.

It is also what makes many of the public love the royals, turning out days in advance and sleeping rough to catch a passing glimpse of a waving hand or wonderful hat at a special occasion.

Sometimes it goes too far. Racegoers at Ascot were warned by security men if they got their mobiles out in the Winners' Enclosure after one of the Queen's horses was victorious.

It was not so much the actuality of the warnings – few would argue that the Queen should not enjoy her moment, more the way it was reported.

With astonishingly outdated pomposity, the BBC descended back into the years of subservience, noting that the crowd were giving a 'knowing touch on the arm' if their phone appeared.

'Commoners – know your place.'

But for a modern royal like Kate it is hard to know whether she is proud, amused, bemused or embarrassed by some of the trappings that come with joining the royal family.

It is probably a mixture of all.

She is, of course, a duchess. Some claim that she would rather have been a princess, but to most of us, the title Duchess of Cambridge is fine. Let's not forget that she will become Queen when William accedes to the throne.

She has received the Queen Elizabeth Diamond Jubilee Medal and the interestingly named Tuvalu Order of Merit. This is, as we all know, the highest award of the tiny nation.

One would have thought that just the pleasure of visiting the tiny Commonwealth Island, which is a gem of the Pacific, would be enough. Still, you can't say no.

Kate is also a Canadian Ranger and, perhaps thanks to her parents' work with on commercial aircraft, an Air Commandant of the Air Training Corps (Honorary).

This award, though, might not have been thought through – it is hoped that it doesn't lead to arguments over who would fly the royal chopper.

One of the perks of being a royal, which they certainly couldn't manage without, is the award of a Coat of Arms.

Kate has two, a personal and a married one. The personal Coat hawks back to days gone by, impaling that of her father with the Coat of her husband.

In fact, Michael Middleton and Prince William get on well, there is no impaling involved, metaphorical of otherwise.

Kate also has her Conjugal Coat of Arms, which is not as libidinous as it sounds. It actually features just the couple's individual arms side by side.

As significant today as those duties sanctioned by the Palace, are the informal ones that people expect.

Kate is seen as a fashion icon, and is criticized if she does not live up to this. We know from her time in Anglesey that she likes nothing more than to dress down.

But when out and about on engagements, public of private, the expectation is that she will be dressed to kill.

As much as this might have caused tensions with the palace, it is what her public expect.

Her dress sense is recognized through numerous awards.

She has been awarded 'Best Newcomer' (a while ago now) by the Telegraph and has appeared twice in People Magazine.

Vanity Fair, Style.com and Buzzword have all featured her and she was on the cover of Vogue's centenary issue.

The Tatler placed her eighth in its top ten lists, which probably says more about the magazine than the Duchess.

Mind you, she wasn't a Duchess when Tatler made its call – the title would have been worth a place or two.

Her profile has been maintained by popular culture although, as we have seen, not always in the fairest or most positive way.

William and Kate were the subjects of a 'factionalized' American TV film called, with startling originality, William and Kate.

Mind you, Americans have a record when it comes to dumbing down the titles of films about the royals.

The story goes that when Alan Bennett's stage plays, The Madness of George III, was to be turned into a film, much consternation was caused over the title.

Producers were terrified that audiences would not attend, as they hadn't seen the prequels, The Madness of George I and II.

Whether this is true is a matter of opinion. It would be great if it was. Whatever, the film was released under the title 'The Madness of King George'.

Catching on to the marketing opportunities of a film about the couple, another was made – this time named William and Catherine: A Royal Romance.

Several documentaries have been made about her as an individual and her relationship with William.

But, Kate would have known that she had made it as a popular icon when the results of a survey were published in 2014.

Young adults from overseas were asked to name the people they most associated with UK culture.

Shakespeare, The Beatles, JK Rowling, David Beckham and, along with the Queen, Kate Middleton.

Looking Forward

Kate Middleton came from a wealthy and privileged background, with committed (some might unfairly conclude pushy) parents and a quiet strength of character.

But she is not a blue blood. Whilst this does not make her unique it is unusual for those joining the inner circle of the royal family.

What she has brought, along with her husband and his brother, is a desire to modernize the monarchy.

In many ways, it is easier for Harry and William to achieve this; they have after all, a direct blood line to the House of Windsor.

But the public possesses a fascination with the wives of future kings, and Kate has tried to use that to do good and to bring about change.

At the same time, she also wants to be a mum, and have her own life.

They are not unreasonable ambitions.

Humans are flawed, and that includes the rich and the royals.

In days gone not too distantly by, people were meant to bow before the Heads of State, to doff their hats and be subservient.

The palace guarded every piece of news as though it were the crown jewels, to be closely watched and let out only in protected glimpses.

In those days, the royal family still committed indiscretions. There was still infidelity, and more. It is just that, apart from the most serious happenings, such as the Wallace Simpson affair, nobody knew.

But, for good or bad, today is different. We are all photographers and film makers, able to capture every moment of any incident on our mobiles.

News sources are immense, not just the national papers and television. But those agencies now compete with the spread of online sources, and that has made them, like a hungry lion, merciless.

In those circumstances, somebody in the public eye has such limited privacy. That extends to her family as well.

And, let's be honest, some of the less responsible media outlets, in the absence of anything newsworthy, just make it up.

Those are the conditions that Kate Middleton lives in. Many will say that she made that choice, and it is right, she did.

But why shouldn't she? We don't ask to fall in love.

Time will tell whether William and Kate go on to become King and Queen, or whether there is some truth about the state of their marriage in the unsubstantiated gossip.

Time will tell how many children she has, and how they grow up. Will little George become king? Many of us, though, will probably not live to see that day.

Time will tell the legacy Kate establishes.

But for now, it would be good to let the mother of two young children, who gives much to the nation already, have a bit of space and privacy.

Printed in Great Britain
by Amazon

This would run through their education, giving them a small chance of enjoying some of the joys and challenges of school and university away from prying eyes.

Certainly, the boys had to cope with constant security, but, in return for the occasional managed story and photo session, they could get on with the early parts of their lives in relative quiet.

Something neither Charles nor, especially, Diana had enjoyed once they had met.

Kate and William, independently of the other, each opted to spend their first year at the University in the halls of residence.